YOUR re
could ap
in our n
cookbo

Share your tried & true family favorites with us instantly at
www.gooseberrypatch.com

If you'd rather jot 'em down by hand, just mail this form to...
Gooseberry Patch • Cookbooks – Call for Recipes
PO Box 812 • Columbus, OH 43216-0812

If your recipe is selected for a book, you'll receive a FREE copy!

Please share only your original recipes or those that you have made your own over the years.

Recipe Name:

Number of Servings:

Any fond memories about this recipe? Special touches you like to add
or handy shortcuts?

Ingredients (include specific measurements):

Instructions (continue on back if needed):

Special Code: **cookbookspage**

Over ↗

Extra space for recipe if needed:

Tell us about yourself...

Your complete contact information is needed so that we can send you your FREE cookbook, if your recipe is published. Phone numbers and email addresses are kept private and will only be used if we have questions about your recipe.

Name:

Address:

City: State: Zip:

Email:

Daytime Phone:

Thank you! Vickie & Jo Ann

★ FOOLPROOF ★
Christmas

Gooseberry Patch

An imprint of Globe Pequot
246 Goose Lane
Guilford, CT 06437

www.gooseberrypatch.com

1•800•854•6673

Copyright 2018, Gooseberry Patch 978-1-62093-280-3

Do you have a tried & true recipe...

tip, craft or memory that you'd like to see featured in
a **Gooseberry Patch** cookbook? Visit our website at
www.gooseberrypatch.com and follow the
easy steps to submit your favorite family recipe.
Or send them to us at:

Gooseberry Patch
PO Box 812
Columbus, OH 43216-0812

Don't forget to include the number of servings your recipe makes,
plus your name, address, phone number and email address. If we
select your recipe, your name will appear right along with it...
and you'll receive a **FREE** copy of the book!

Contents

Dedication

For those who love every minute of the holiday season, from baking the first tray of cookies to unwrapping the very last gift.

Appreciation

A warm thanks to everyone who shared their best recipes for can't-miss holiday dishes!

SWEET CHRISTMAS
Memories

Countdown to Christmas

Hollie Moots
Marysville, OH

From the time my boys were toddlers, we always did a Christmas countdown in the form of a paper chain. Each day from the first of December on would have an activity or surprise for them. We strung it across the banister of our loft. The excitement grew as the chain shrank! There was never anything fancy, just simple treats like each boy getting to pick dinner and help Mommy cook, a night to go see Christmas lights, or family game night, but they always came running down the hall in the morning to see what was in store for the day! It was such a fun way to stretch out the excitement of the holiday season and enjoy it as a family. After many years of this, though, I decided they were probably too old for it. Electronics and clothes had replaced toys on their wish lists...my boys were growing up. December first came and we were bustling around the house, getting ready for work and school. My 12-year-old son came to me with a puzzled look and asked, "Mom, where's the countdown chain?" I told him I just assumed they had outgrown it and wouldn't want to do those things anymore. His face was so sad! He told me he and his brother had talked about it before bed the night before and couldn't wait to see what today held! I apologized and promised them a countdown by that evening. As I hurried to put it together that day, I was so touched and humbled that something that seemed so simple had meant so much to them. Not the expensive gifts or the lavish decorations... but the very simple paper countdown to Christmas chain that I'd created as a young mother. We switched to doing just the "Twelve Days of Christmas" when they got a bit older. Last year they were both away at college, so it was the first year that we didn't do some kind of countdown. They both talk about the fond memories and traditions we built, though. I hope they continue these with their own families some day.

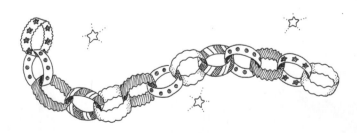

A Christmas Chill

Geri Meuschke
Acworth, GA

When our children were growing up, we would all go to the Christmas tree farm or local nursery to choose the "perfect" Christmas tree. Once when we got home, the tree would not fit through the front door, so back to the nursery! Another time, the tree had absolutely the straightest trunk, but when we got home the tree was so crooked it would not fit in the stand without a major trimming of the limbs. After the kids had all left for college, we moved from Missouri to Georgia. It was just the two of us on a warm December day at the local nursery, choosing the "perfect" tree once again. The store had a huge display of flocked trees, and when I stepped into the greenhouse, a sudden chill overcame me! I hurriedly tried to find my husband to share this experience with him. There he stood in the middle. As I approached him, he asked, "Do you feel cold?" We went home with the perfect tree that day.

Celebrating Christmas Past, Present and Future

Monica Britt
Fairdale, WV

I love to host themed Christmas parties. Over the years, we've had a snowman party, an ugly Christmas sweater party and a Grinch party, just to name a few. This past year was my favorite! We had a Dickens-themed Christmas party, complete with all the decorations. We put up three trees in our family room. One tree was decorated with antique red glass ornaments and picture frames holding black and white photos of loved ones to represent Christmas Past. The middle tree was over ten feet tall, and decorated with pine cones, clear bulbs, big bows made of red and black checked ribbon, and ornaments that looked like gift packages to represent Christmas Present. The third tree was adorned with white bulbs, wooden ornaments (such as ice skates) to represent adventures that await us, and words like peace and joy to symbolize Christmas Future. That evening our family gathered together ready to celebrate, wearing matching flannel shirts for festive picture taking. Grandparents told stories of the good old days, aunts and uncles chatted about current family updates and young couples shared their plans for the future. We all enjoyed a menu that consisted of traditional family recipes like Aunt Tish's Cheese Ball, current favorites like BBQ Sliders, and new recipes like Slow-Cooker Macaroni & Cheese. It was a special occasion filled with delicious food, joyful Christmas carol singing, lots of laughter, sweet reminiscing and many new memories!

Santa Rides a Motorcycle

Sandy Coffey
Cincinnati, OH

A few years ago, we headed over with our four kids to Grandma's apartment on Christmas Eve day. As we were pulling into the lot, a Santa pulled in on a motorcycle as well. We got into the building and headed for the elevator, as did Santa. Following us off the elevator and down the hall, he also entered Grandma's apartment, plopping down in her chair. After a little chat with her, he got up and left. Our kids were wide-eyed and astonished. Had they been good? Lo and behold, it was their Uncle Lynn. He rode the motorcycle every Christmas Eve day to visit folks. The kids did not know this for years...they got such a kick out of Santa riding a motorcycle!

Santa's Boots

Kim Kilonsky
Taylor, PA

My father was a fireman, and he usually worked the night shift on Christmas Eve. To add to our anticipation, my brother and I had to wait for Dad to get home from work on Christmas morning and eat breakfast with him before commencing with the gift opening. Mom always had a good laugh watching us "suffer" through it. The best part was that we always found our stockings inside "Santa's boots"...which in fact were my father's fireman boots. It is a tradition I've since passed on to my children as well.

I Believe in Santa

Helen Thoen
Manly, IA

The Christmas that I am going to tell you about happened in the early 1950s and is the first Christmas I remember. I was not quite four years old that Christmas Eve, when Santa visited our farm home and personally delivered presents. Mom and I were in the living room when we heard the sound of sleigh bells coming closer and closer. Suddenly Santa bounded into the room in all his crimson glory and he did indeed have a bundle flung on his back. The whole room sparkled with magic and wonder. Santa knelt on one knee to undo his pack. He reached into it and brought out gifts for me. I didn't want to get any closer than necessary to receive those gifts, so I stretched my arms out to Santa and quickly handed each one to my mom standing by my side. Santa gave me a doll with a pretty blue doll bed and a beautiful blue quilt to go on it. How I wished my dad could see all of this! But Mom assured me that he was outside helping Santa by holding onto his sleigh and reindeer so they wouldn't get away. Then in a twinkling, as quickly as he had come, he was gone. When I was older, I discovered a mask with a long white beard and other parts of a Santa outfit tucked away in our attic. It turned out that Dad had made the doll bed and Mom made the doll quilt. I still have both of them. That dear Santa of long ago is no longer with us, but my cherished memories will remain with me forever.

Sugar Coma Cookies

Margarquet Fortunato
Grand Marais, MN

Every year, our family gets together for a wonderful tradition that was born when our kids were pretty small. It started out as an accident, and it turned into something that makes us all smile when we talk about past Christmas memories. We have a "sugar coma" cookie decorating contest. When the kids were little, we started the tradition of making sugar cookies and putting them out with a big glass of milk for Santa on Christmas Eve, along with some reindeer food, of course! One year, our girls got carried away with the decorating and over-iced and over-sprinkled some cookies. When it came time to choosing what cookies to leave Santa that evening, our girls decided that the over-iced cookies were the prettiest and that Santa would like them most of all. Over the years, we've had categories of Prettiest, Messiest, Most Icing and Most Likely To Give You a Tummyache. Since then, our girls have grown up and have families of their own, but the tradition remains, and I'm happy to say our children have passed this fun activity on to our grandchildren now. It's also been a big hit at the annual holiday party we host here at home every year. The younger kids are kept very busy decorating and eating their creations. We give them goodie bags to take the rest home for them to share with their loved ones...and even with Santa, we've heard!

Christmas Snow Bunnies

Renee Barton
La Porte, IN

One Christmas, my aunt and uncle drove up from Ohio to our home in Michigan. We couldn't wait for them to arrive! We had just gotten a huge snowfall and were excited to go out and make snowmen with them. Once my aunt and uncle arrived, we started to pester them to come out and play. My aunt wanted to take a rest and freshen up, so Mom bundled us up and sent us outside to play for awhile to get us out of their hair. When they came out, I remember being so excited I was jumping up and down. Not only had my aunt and uncle come out to play, so did my parents! We started rolling snowballs for a snowman. We kept rolling and rolling until we had two humongous snowballs. They were too big to pick up, so we ended up making two snowmen instead. As we got the second and third balls up on top, we discovered that they were well over six feet tall. My mom and my aunt decided we needed to make them into snow bunnies instead. So they put big ears on them and my mom mixed up some food coloring for us to "paint" their ears pink. Our snow bunnies had big eyes, whiskers made from branches and carrot noses, which I thought were the funniest things. They were the hit of the neighborhood, and best of all, they were made with love by the whole family.

SWEET CHRISTMAS
Memories

Cold Winter Fun

Deborah Patterson
Carmichael, CA

When I was very young, we lived in Rouses Point, New York, one mile from the Canadian border. To say it was cold in the wintertime is an understatement! My four sisters and I really did walk to school in the winter blasts of the late 1950s. It was terribly cold, and we tried to run to the house from our school. One of the most fun things that we used to do (it'd be outlawed now!) was when my father tied the sled to the back bumper of our car. Then he pulled us for a ride on the sled, up and down the snowy, icy street. It was tricky to stay on the sled when the car stopped, but we never did bump into it. Once, my dad made me a giant snow tunnel that was like an igloo. I spent many hours in the tunnel, pretending to be the princess of the castle. A hot cup of chocolate was always waiting for us when we came up for air. Those were the times we used our imagination to keep ourselves busy. My father is gone now, but the memories remain clear as day. Somehow we recovered from the sled rides and snow tunnels, and now they bring pleasant memories each winter to each of us.

Childhood Santa

Maryann Brett
Johnstown, PA

My favorite Christmas memory started in the late 1960s when I
was just six or seven years old. My family of seven moved from a
two-bedroom house into a four-bedroom house, and we needed a lot
of new furniture. With their purchase of furniture, my parents were
lucky enough to get a life-size, six-foot, light-up Santa Claus...free!
That Santa was larger than life when I first saw him, standing so much
taller than me. Every year, Dad would tie him to our porch to keep
him in place, then turn on his light for all to see. We moved again in
my teenage years, and Mom made sure that Santa came with us.
Several years later, when I was married and had a house of my own,
I was given Santa for my own family to enjoy. My husband would
tie Santa to our porch just like Dad had done when I was a young girl.
Over the years, old age and the elements have taken their toll on my
beloved Santa. The hard plastic became brittle and moving him became
difficult. Many times my husband told me this would be his last year,
and when his boot fell off and he could no longer stand, I feared the
worst. Not willing to give up on the Santa I had treasured for almost
my entire life, I came up with a new way to still enjoy him. Santa
now lives all year long in my attic, in a box sturdy enough to support
his legs. Every December, I very gently slide the box in front of the
attic window and turn on his light. There he stands, still bigger than
life, until Christmas Eve. That Santa is 50 years old now. His warm
glow on these cold Pennsylvania winter nights never fails to warm
my heart!

SWEET CHRISTMAS
Memories

Tree Skirt Keepsake

Jean Kontny
Hartford, WI

When my first son was born, I was young and didn't have a lot of money for Christmas decorations and such. I bought a large piece of quilted fabric, cut it into a circle for a tree skirt and sewed a binding around the edges. I traced my baby's hand, cut it out of a piece of felt and embroidered his name and the year on it. Then I sewed it onto the tree skirt. The following Christmas, I did his handprint again, and added his baby brother's to it, as well. Now, more than 30 years later, I have all five of my kids' handprints from over the the years and am working on those of my eight grandchildren. It's truly a precious and treasured keepsake!

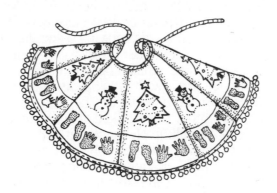

Grammie for Christmas!

Amy Linderman
Wickliffe, OH

Every Christmas morning, my mom tells the same sweet story while we eat breakfast. When we were small, on Christmas morning my twin sister Julie and I would come down the stairs together. There would be the beautifully lit Christmas tree, the stuffed stockings and presents piled underneath the tree. My mom would ask, "What do you see, girls?" and we would say "Grammie!" and run to our grandmother first, before looking at anything else.

Christmas Memories 1939

Alice Joy Randall
Nacogdoches, TX

These are my sister Jo Nell's memories as told to me. She would have been five years old on December 29 that year. It was my third Christmas and our brother Paul's first, as he was seven months old. That was the year Jo Nell found all her gifts ahead of time, hidden in a trunk. Although I was too young to remember any of this, I do have vague memories of the house in Crosby, Texas where we lived. Jo Nell was feeling rather sad because Mama and Papa (our maternal grandparents, who lived in San Augustine, Texas) weren't going to get to come to Crosby this Christmas. But later on, they decided they would come after all and took the bus to our house. We were all waiting on the front porch when the bus drove up. Jo Nell still remembers the "swoosh" of the air brakes. Papa was carrying a big tricycle in one hand and Mama was carrying a smaller one...one for my sister and one for me! I remember the tricycles well. Jo Nell and I each received a truck too. Hers was a Coca-Cola truck with little bottles of Coke. Mine was an ice truck with little blocks of ice and a pair of tiny ice tongs. We really liked our trucks! They must have been something special, for Mother often talked about them in later years. We both received dolls as well. Jo Nell took her doll by the hand and rode it around on her tricycle, with the doll's feet dragging the ground until they got dirty, and Mother suggested she put the doll on her bed. The baby book Mother kept for me says that I received a ball and a toy bugle as well. Such wonderful Christmas memories!

Christmas Eve Surprise

Susi Downs
Jacksonville, NC

Every year on Christmas Eve, our family went out to a fancy restaurant for dinner. Halfway through the meal, my father would say he'd forgotten his cigarettes. Of course, he had to go get some more, so he would leave. When we got home, Christmas presents would be under the tree, as Santa had come. One year, we went out to dinner and my father didn't get up to leave. My mother was getting antsy. She just thought they would put out the presents that night. When we got home, lo and behold, there were presents under the tree! Even my mother was surprised, and that made it extra special. Our neighbors, who were very good friends, had put out the presents for my father. It was fantastic and wonderful.

Christmas Hats for All

Karla Himpelmann
Mount Pleasant, MI

My mother-in-law Dorothy always felt she had to have something for everyone to open on Christmas. Dorothy had eight children and 18 grandchildren to buy for, and we all told her that she didn't have to do this. She didn't spend a lot on any one gift. It was always interesting to see what unique presents everyone was unwrapping. One year, instead of buying gifts at the stores, she had a lady from church make knitted stocking hats for all 18 grandchildren and their spouses, too, for those who were married. Her friend made all of the hats in just a few weeks' time before Christmas. It was so much fun, watching as each person opened their gift of a hat. They weren't all the same color, either! The kids all enjoyed their useful gifts. Even though Dorothy passed away a couple years ago, these hats still get mentioned at the holidays. Some of the kids still have their hat and the photo with the group all wearing them.

Lucky Christmas Party Apron

Janis Parr
Ontario, Canada

I always host a Christmas potluck dinner or a cookie exchange for family & friends before Christmas. One year I was trying to think of something different that would be fun to do at the party. I have a collection of aprons...my mom's, some new, some vintage. As each guest arrived, I invited them to choose an apron to wear during the party. I can still hear their giggles now, as they held up each apron to decide which one suited them and which would fit as they tried them on. Little did they know that I had sewed a tiny Christmas button far down on the corner of one apron, well out of sight. After we finished eating, I asked everyone to check the skirt of their apron for anything unusual. The guest with the Christmas button-apron won a prize...two jars of my homemade jam and a Gooseberry Patch booklet. What a fun way to create memories!

Christmas Eve Drive

Patricia Taylor
Louisville, KY

On Christmas Eve when I was little, my father, mother, teenage sister and I would get into my father's big blue '67 Buick to see the Christmas lights. I remember the air would be so cold, but the Buick was toasty warm. At that time, most people didn't decorate with a lot of lawn decorations, just colorful lights on the house. At one home nearby, though, the family decorated with a Nativity scene, lights all around the house and Santa Claus with his reindeer on top of the house. How beautiful it looked as we drove past in our warm car! I would use my red mitten to clean off the fogged-up windows. Afterwards, we would come back home. Daddy would put the car in the garage and we would go inside. The lights were left on in our basement. Santa Claus had come to our house! I was scared to go to our den...what if he was still there? My sister coaxed me to come and I slowly crept down the stairs. I saw the lit-up Santa face on the wall. As I turned the corner to our Christmas tree, I saw that Santa had left all the gifts under the tree. The looks on my parents' and sister's faces are still in my memory.

A Memorable Gift

Kathy Rigg
Mount Sterling, IL

One year at Christmastime, I really wanted to surprise my mother with something unusual. We live in the same town, so I had to enlist my dad's help, but he was all in the task. I purchased an inexpensive 12-piece Nativity set. I wrapped each piece and labeled the first package with "On the first day of Christmas, my true love gave to me", the second with "The second day of Christmas..." and so on. I counted backwards from Christmas Day and saved the Baby Jesus to be given to her on Christmas. Dad put the packages on the front porch, in the mailbox, on the window ledge. Mom thought she knew who was leaving the gifts, but actually had forgotten about it when I arrived and the last package was attached to another gift. She was so surprised, as she'd never suspected Dad or me! Mom still displays that Nativity set every year.

Opening Gifts with Grandma

Kristi Edney
Bowie, MD

When I was growing up, my grandmother was my best friend. My siblings and I were "Army brats" and weren't always around for the holidays. The Christmas I remember the best was when we all got to open our presents first...five brothers and a sister, five cousins...and Grandma waited through all of them. Then, before we could go play with our new toys, we had to sit and wait for Grandma to open all of her own presents. She would use a letter opener to take the paper off. She didn't want to tear it, she wanted to use it again & again. We thought she'd never get done! I have that letter opener today, and I use it to open my letters from my world-wide pen pals.

Sneak a Peek!

Melissa Dattoli
Richmond, VA

In the house I grew up in, the living room and my bedroom were separated by a long hallway. Every Christmas, I would try to sneak into the living room while everyone else was still asleep, to see what gifts Santa had left. Every year, my father would set up some sort of obstacle to keep me from getting into the living room early. It was always fun trying to get by whatever carefully laid traps he had set down that hallway. I laugh every time I think back to those Christmases! There were baby gates stacked three high on top of each other, covered in jingle bells. Fishing line made for a great trip-wire, strategically placed around my room and tied to anything that would make a loud noise as it fell. The best year was the one where he set a motion sensor up in my bedroom doorway. It was wired to a stereo, with a loud recording of sirens blaring and his voice saying, "Get back in your bed!" Some Christmases I managed to get by his traps, and some years he'd catch me trapped in that hallway wearing my Christmas pajamas and a look of pure defeat. I will remember those Christmases forever. My parents always made the holidays special in little ways like these, and the memories are more precious to me than any gifts.

Christmas Eve Picnic

Susan Church
Crete, NE

Our church's Christmas Eve service is held at 5:30 pm, and the church is about a 30-minute drive from home. When our boys were young, that was too early for dinner to be served, and too late for a full meal when we got home. So one Christmas Eve, I fixed hors d'oeuvres-type foods that could all be ready when we got home from church, things like cocktail sausages in barbecue sauce, cheese cubes and apple slices with dip. I also made a special fizzy punch with white grape juice and ginger ale, served in pretty Christmas stemware. A blanket was spread on the floor in front of the Christmas tree, with all lights off except the Christmas lights. Christmas music was playing softly in the background. Then we all sat on the floor for our "picnic". The boys thought it was so wonderful to be able to eat on the floor with the lights off! So the next year, they asked if we were going to have our picnic again...and thus a tradition was born! Our boys are now 28 and 25, and our Christmas Eve picnic is as important to all of us now as then, maybe more so.

Homemade is Best for Christmas

Sharon Laney
Maryville, TN

My mother lived by the old English saying, "Necessity is the mother of invention." For weeks before Christmas, we would hear her old treadle sewing machine humming us to sleep. She sewed new wardrobes for our dolls and sometimes a Christmas dress to match ours. One year she ordered new doll wigs the color of our hair. I was the only brunette among three blondes and felt very special. She also drew paper dolls for us, and we cut clothes out of old catalogs to dress them. The example of her creativity and ingenuity was the best gift she ever gave us. To this day, I enjoy giving and receiving homemade gifts...I know the time and love that goes into them.

COZY
HOLIDAY
Breakfasts

Stuffed French Toast Casserole

Sara Redeker
Grand Haven, MI

I first tasted this delicious overnight casserole one morning when my boss made breakfast for us. So good, I couldn't stop eating it! Now I make it for my family on cold winter mornings, especially at Christmastime.

10 slices bread, crusts removed
2 8-oz. pkgs. cream cheese, cubed
1/2 lb. cooked ham, cubed

1 doz. eggs, beaten
2 c. milk
1/3 c. pancake syrup
Optional: additional syrup

Cut bread into cubes. Layer half of the bread cubes evenly in a greased 13"x9" baking pan. Scatter cream cheese and ham over top. Layer with remaining bread; set aside. In a large bowl, whisk together eggs, milk and syrup. Pour over bread mixture, making sure it soaks into the bread. Cover with aluminum foil; refrigerate overnight. Uncover; bake at 350 degrees for 40 to 45 minutes, until bubbly and eggs are set. Serve with more syrup, if desired. Serves 6 to 8.

Celebrate the season with a holiday brunch buffet for friends & neighbors! It's a joyful time of year to renew old acquaintances while sharing scrumptious food together.

Breakfasts

Weekend Ham & Egg Skillet

Gladys Kielar
Whitehouse, OH

This is a delicious skillet dish that's great for brunch or even for dinner. We enjoy it on weekend mornings.

1 T. butter	1 c. cooked ham, cubed
3 potatoes, peeled and diced	3 eggs, beaten
1/4 c. onion, chopped	salt and pepper to taste
1/4 c. green pepper, chopped	1 c. shredded Cheddar cheese

Melt butter in a skillet over medium heat. Add potatoes; sauté until tender and golden. Add onion and green pepper; sauté until tender-crisp. Add ham to skillet; reduce heat to medium-low. In a bowl, whisk together eggs, salt and pepper; pour over ingredients in skillet. Top with cheese. Cook, stirring occasionally, until eggs are completely set. Serves 4.

A Christmas wreath for breakfast! Simply arrange refrigerated cinnamon rolls on a baking sheet in a wreath shape and bake as usual. Frost and decorate with candied cherries.

Make-Ahead Scrambled Eggs

Angela Murphy
Tempe, AZ

Eggs for the whole family! So handy...do all the egg-cracking and scrambling ahead of time, then just pop in the oven later. I fry up some bacon while the eggs are baking. No need to watch two skillets!

1 doz. eggs, beaten
1/2 c. half-and-half
1/4 t. salt
1/8 t. pepper

2 T. butter
3/4 c. sour cream
1 c. shredded Cheddar cheese,
    divided

In a large bowl, whisk together eggs, half-and-half, salt and pepper; set aside. Melt butter in a large skillet over medium heat; pour egg mixture into skillet. Cook, stirring gently, until eggs are scrambled and just set, but still moist. Remove from heat; stir in sour cream and 1/2 cup cheese. Transfer egg mixture to a buttered 13"x9" glass baking pan. Sprinkle with remaining cheese; cover tightly and refrigerate. To serve, uncover; bake at 350 degrees for 20 to 30 minutes, until warmed through. Makes 6 to 8 servings.

Mashed Potato Cake

Janae Mallonee
Marlboro, MA

This is a great way to use up leftover mashed potatoes. We make it for breakfast, or as a side dish for dinner. My aunt made these, mixing in some leftover sweet potatoes. That sounds good too!

2 c. mashed potatoes
1 egg, beaten
2 t. all-purpose flour
salt and pepper to taste

oil for frying
Optional: shredded Cheddar
    cheese, sliced green onions,
    bacon bits

In a bowl, mix together potatoes, egg, flour and seasonings. Add a little more flour if mixture is too thin. Form into a large, flat patty. Warm 1/2 inch oil in a skillet over medium-high heat. Carefully add patty to hot oil; cook until golden. Turn; cook other side. Cut into wedges; add toppings, if desired. Serves 4.

Chocolate Chip Coffee Cake

Jo Ann
Gooseberry Patch

*I love this easy coffee cake recipe...you will too! It goes together
in minutes and makes enough for a family gathering,
a church reception or everyone in the office.*

18-1/2 oz. pkg. yellow cake mix   3 eggs, beaten
8-oz. container sour cream   3/4 c. water

Combine all ingredients in a large bowl. Beat with an electric mixer on
low speed until moistened. Turn to high speed; beat for 2 minutes, or
until well mixed. Spread 2/3 of batter in a greased and lightly floured
13"x9" baking pan. Sprinkle with half of Streusel Topping. Repeat
layering with remaining batter and topping. Bake at 350 degrees for
35 to 45 minutes, until a toothpick inserted in the center tests done.
Makes 16 servings.

Streusel Topping:

1 c. brown sugar, packed   1/2 c. semi-sweet chocolate
2 T. all-purpose flour   chips
2 T. butter, melted   1/2 c. chopped walnuts
2 t. cinnamon

Combine all ingredients in a bowl; mix well.

Headed to a Christmas Eve gathering? Take along a fresh-baked
coffee cake for the hostess...a thoughtful timesaver she'll
appreciate Christmas morning!

Cinnamon Roll-Ups

Joan White
Malvern, PA

Kids love these yummy treats, and they'll enjoy helping you put them together for baking. Adults enjoy them with hot coffee.

8-oz. pkg. cream cheese,
  softened
1 egg yolk, beaten
1-1/4 c. sugar, divided

18 to 20 slices white bread
1/2 c. butter, melted
1 T. cinnamon

In a small bowl, combine cream cheese, egg yolk and 1/4 cup sugar; mix well and set aside. Flatten bread with a rolling pin. Spread cream cheese mixture over each slice to within 1/2-inch from edges. Roll up slices diagonally from point to point. Place melted butter in a shallow bowl; combine cinnamon and remaining sugar in another bowl. Dip roll-ups into butter, then into cinnamon-sugar; arrange on an ungreased baking sheet. Bake at 350 degrees for 16 to 19 minutes, until lightly golden. Makes 18 to 20 roll-ups.

A fun countdown to Christmas! Get the family together during breakfast and think up 25 fun holiday activities like making gingerbread cookies for classmates, dancing to holiday music, sledding or reading a Christmas story. Write each on a paper strip, link them together, then pull one off each day in December and do the activity together.

Cinnamon Waffles

Aubrey Nygren
Farmington, NM

We love waffles, so I decided to try a new twist on the usual waffle recipe. It was a hit and made the house smell oh-so yummy. Delicious with butter and maple syrup, or for a special treat, top with fresh peaches and whipped cream.

1-3/4 c. all-purpose flour
2 T. sugar
1 T. baking powder
1 t. cinnamon
1/4 t. salt

2 eggs
1-3/4 c. milk
1/2 c. butter, melted
1 t. vanilla extract

In a large bowl, stir together flour, sugar, baking powder, cinnamon and salt. Make a well in center of flour mixture; set aside. In another bowl, beat eggs lightly; stir in milk, melted butter and vanilla. Add egg mixture all at once to well in flour mixture. Stir just until moistened; batter should be slightly lumpy. For each waffle, pour one to 1-1/4 cups of batter onto a preheated, lightly greased waffle iron. Bake according to manufacturer's directions. Makes 4 to 6 waffles.

Hosting a brunch buffet? Offer a variety of syrups, butter, jams and jellies on a small table that's separate from the serving table. Everyone can choose their favorite toppings while the buffet line keeps moving.

Holiday Breakfast

Judy Lange
Imperial, PA

So delicious and so easy! Serve on Christmas morning,
Easter morning or sleepover mornings.

1 lb. ground pork breakfast
   sausage, browned and
   drained
1 doz. eggs, lightly beaten

2 c. whole milk
1-1/2 c. shredded Cheddar
   cheese
5-oz. pkg. seasoned croutons

Mix all ingredients together in a large bowl. Transfer to a lightly greased 13"x9" inch baking pan. Bake, uncovered, at 350 degrees for 40 to 45 minutes, until eggs are set. Cool for 10 minutes before serving. Makes 6 to 8 servings.

Fresh fruit salad is a scrumptious, healthy side that just about everyone will love. Slice up oranges, strawberries and kiwi fruit and toss with a simple dressing made of equal parts honey and lemon or orange juice.

Cheesy Potluck Potatoes

Mary Lou Thomas
Portland, ME

My go-to recipe brunch! Be sure to use the refrigerated (not frozen) potatoes from the dairy case.

20-oz. pkg. refrigerated
   shredded hashbrowns
10-3/4 oz. can cream of potato
   soup
1 c. shredded Cheddar cheese

1/2 c. milk
1/2 c. green onions, sliced
1 T. butter, melted
1 t. garlic, finely chopped

In a large bowl, combine all ingredients; stir to mix well. Spread in a lightly greased 8"x8" baking pan. Bake, uncovered, at 350 degrees for 55 to 60 minutes, until potatoes are tender and center is heated through. Makes 6 to 8 servings.

Vintage salt & pepper shakers, in the shape of snowmen
or Mr. & Mrs. Santa, add a touch of holiday cheer to
any table and a smile to guests' faces.

Nanny's Cranberry Biscuit Ring
Kay Veara
Jonesboro, AR

This is a recipe from my mother-in-law, who lived to the age of 93. My husband and I have been married more than 40 years. In our earlier married life, this was a breakfast treat that we enjoyed often when we visited "Nanny & Papa" on their farm in Florida. A very pretty treat for Christmas Eve or Christmas morning.

1/3 c. butter, melted
1/4 c. honey
1/2 c. whole-berry cranberry
    sauce

2 7-1/2 oz. tubes refrigerated
    biscuits

Spread butter in the bottom of a Bundt® pan; add honey and cranberry sauce. Stand biscuits on their side, forming a ring around pan. Bake at 350 degrees for 12 to 15 minutes, until biscuits are set and lightly golden. Cover pan with a plate; turn biscuits out onto plate. Spoon out any remaining topping, spreading evenly over biscuits. Serves 5 to 6.

Winter Hot Chocolate
Shannon Reents
Bellville, OH

The perfect way to warm up after sledding or shoveling snow! We take it along to football games too. Melted marshmallows give this a homemade creamy and frothy texture that my family loves.

4 c. milk
2 T. baking cocoa
8 t. sugar

1-1/2 c. mini marshmallows
Garnish: whipped cream topping

In a saucepan, combine milk, cocoa, sugar and marshmallows. Cook and stir over medium heat until hot and marshmallows are melted, about 8 minutes. Do not boil. Remove from heat; ladle into mugs and serve topped with whipped cream. Serves 4.

Dress up mugs of hot cocoa with
candy cane stirrers.

Breakfasts

Auntie Char's Overnight Brunch Eggs

Gretchen Brown
Hillsboro, OR

My Auntie Char shared this easy recipe years ago. Now I make it every Christmas Eve, then in the morning I can just pop it in the oven. By the time we're done opening gifts, it's ready to serve.

8 eggs, beaten
2 c. milk
8-oz. pkg. shredded yellow
   Cheddar cheese, divided
8-oz. pkg. shredded white
   Cheddar cheese, divided

8 slices bread, crusts removed,
   cubed
1 lb. mild ground pork breakfast
   sausage, browned and
   drained

Whisk together eggs and milk in a large bowl; set aside. Combine cheeses in another bowl; set aside. To assemble, arrange bread cubes in the bottom of a lightly greased 13"x9" baking pan. Top bread with sausage, 3/4 of cheese mixture, egg mixture and remaining cheese. Cover with aluminum foil and refrigerate overnight. Uncover; bake at 350 degrees for one hour. Remove from oven; let stand for 10 minutes before serving. Makes 8 servings.

Little extras for Christmas morning...a small wrapped gift at each place setting, soft holiday music in the background and no lights allowed except those on the tree. So magical!

Good-for-You Morning Melts

Wendy Ball
Battle Creek, MI

I used to make these breakfast sandwiches for my husband and myself when we were newly married. It always made our small kitchen warm and cozy with just the two of us. Now I sometimes use bagel thins or sandwich thins instead of English muffins. They turn out a bit crisper, yet still make you feel warm inside.

4 English muffins, split
   and toasted
1 T. Dijon mustard
8 slices Canadian bacon

1-1/2 Honey Crisp or Fuji
   apples, cored and thinly
   sliced
8 slices favorite cheese

Spread cut sides of muffin halves with mustard; place on an ungreased baking sheet. Top each with bacon, apple and cheese slices. Bake at 350 degrees for 6 to 8 minutes, until cheese melts. Serve hot. Makes 4 to 8 servings.

Kris Kringle's Noel Coffee

Julie Ann Perkins
Anderson, IN

Jazz up hot coffee in a twinkling! Perfect for brunch or for sharing with good friends.

6 c. hot coffee
3/4 c. chocolate syrup

1/4 t. cinnamon extract
Garnish: whipped cream

Combine hot coffee, syrup and extract in a large container; stir well. Serve in mugs, topped with a dollop of whipped cream. Makes 6 to 8 servings.

Invite friends over for brunch
before a day of shopping...
a terrific way to start the day!

Breakfasts

Healthy Oatmeal-Raisin Breakfast Cookies

Marsha Baker
Pioneer, OH

We love these cookies with our morning coffee...they're an awesome way to begin a busy day! Could there be a better time of year than Christmas to have cookies for breakfast?

1 c. rolled oats, uncooked
3/4 c. oat flour
2 t. baking powder
3/4 to 1 t. cinnamon
1/2 t. nutmeg
1 t. vanilla extract

1 egg, beaten
3 T. honey or agave nectar
1/4 c. plain Greek yogurt
1/4 c. chopped nuts
1/4 c. raisins or sweetened
   dried cranberries

Add rolled oats to a blender; process until powdery and measure out 3/4 cup. In a bowl, combined processed oats, oat flour, baking powder and spices; mix well. Add vanilla, egg, honey or nectar and yogurt; stir until well blended. Fold in nuts and raisins or cranberries. Spread dough onto parchment paper-lined baking sheets, forming into 4 or 5 large cookies. Shape with spoon and pat down a bit. Bake at 375 degrees for 6 to 10 minutes, until golden. Makes 4 to 5 large cookies.

If you love to bake, keep a small vintage coffee grinder on hand for grinding whole spices. The extra-fresh flavor of freshly ground nutmeg, cinnamon and cloves can't be beat.

Sharon's Lazy Eggs

Sharon Velenosi
Costa Mesa, CA

This easy recipe will remind you of Eggs Benedict. It has been one of our favorites for Christmas breakfast gatherings. Make it an extra-special treat by adding a slice of ham or Canadian bacon to each muffin half.

1 doz. eggs, hard-boiled, peeled
    and quartered
10-3/4 oz. can cream of
    mushroom soup
10-3/4 oz. can cream of
    chicken soup

1 c. milk
1/2 t. Worcestershire sauce
Optional: 10-1/2 oz. can white
    sauce
1 doz. English muffins, split
    and toasted

Arrange quartered eggs in a large casserole dish; set aside. In a saucepan, combine soups, milk, Worcestershire sauce and white sauce, if using. Cook and stir over medium heat until heated through and smooth; pour hot sauce over eggs. To serve, place 2 toasted muffin halves on each plate. Ladle warm egg mixture over muffins. Serves 12.

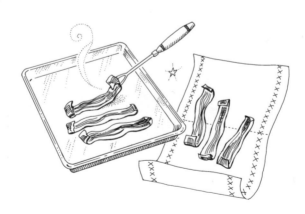

The easiest way ever to make crispy bacon! Place bacon slices on a broiler pan. Bake at 400 degrees for 12 to 15 minutes. Turn bacon over and bake for another 8 to 10 minutes. So simple... why not toss on a few extra slices to garnish a salad?

Janet's Quick Cheese Grits

Janet Reinhart
Columbia, IL

We first tasted this recipe at a church potluck and knew we had to make it ourselves. I've lightened up the calories a little and we've enjoyed making variations by adding 1/4 cup of chopped jalapeños or one to two cloves of chopped garlic, to make it a dinner side dish. I'm sure it would be good with other cheeses too! Enjoy alongside eggs and buttered toast.

1/4 c. butter, sliced
2-1/4 c. milk
3/4 c. quick-cooking grits,
    uncooked

5-oz. jar sharp pasteurized
    process cheese spread
1/2 c. grated Parmesan cheese

Melt butter in a saucepan over medium heat; add milk. Heat just until boiling; do not boil. Sprinkle grits over hot milk mixture, stirring often until creamy. Add cheeses; cook and stir until melted. Transfer to a serving dish; serve warm. Serves 6 for 8.

Use a slow cooker set on low to keep sausage gravy, scrambled eggs or other breakfast foods warm and toasty for brunch.

Cherry Brunch Muffins

Leona Krivda
Belle Vernon, PA

These muffins are really good with hot coffee or tea. If you are invited to brunch, take them along in a napkin-lined basket...sure to be appreciated! Use another flavor of pie filling if you like.

18-1/4 oz. pkg. French vanilla
  cake mix
21-oz. can cherry pie filling

1 c. all-purpose flour
1/2 c. brown sugar, packed
1/2 c. butter, softened

In a large bowl, mix dry cake mix and pie filling. Spoon batter into 12 paper-lined muffin cups, filling 2/3 full; set aside. In a separate bowl, combine flour, brown sugar and butter; stir until crumbly. Sprinkle crumb mixture over muffins. Bake at 350 degrees for 25 minutes. Makes one dozen.

Quick Pineapple Rolls

Carolyn Deckard
Bedford, IN

My oldest daughter loves pineapple, so I always made these for her for breakfast. I hope you'll enjoy these as much as she did!

1/2 c. butter, softened
1 c. brown sugar, packed
20-oz. can crushed pineapple,
  drained

2 7-1/2 oz. tubes refrigerated
  biscuits

Blend butter and brown sugar in a bowl; stir in pineapple. Spoon mixture into a greased 9" round cake pan. Arrange biscuits on top. Bake at 400 degrees for 15 minutes, or until lightly golden. To serve, invert onto a plate. Makes 8 servings.

When Christmas day comes there is still the same warm feeling we had as children, the same warmth that enfolds our hearts and our homes.

–Joan Winmill Brown

Light Blueberry Danish

Molly Ebert
Columbus, IN

This is an old recipe I reworked to make it lower in fat. It's still delicious...just as good as the original!

8-oz. tube refrigerated reduced-
   fat crescent dinner rolls
1/2 c. Neufchâtel or light cream
   cheese, softened

2 T. sugar or powdered
   sweetener
1/2 c. fresh blueberries

Unroll dough into 4 rectangles; firmly press perforations together to seal. In a bowl, blend cheese and sugar; spread onto dough rectangles to within 1/2 inch of edges. Top evenly with blueberries. Bring opposite corners of rectangles together; press together to seal. Place on an ungreased baking sheet. Bake at 375 degrees for 15 to 18 minutes, until golden. Makes 4 servings.

Cinnamon Monkey Bread

Cindy Kemp
Lake Jackson, TX

This is a great rainy-day project for you and the kids. I got this recipe 25 years ago when my daughters were little. They loved making it with me almost as much as eating it! And yes, it does call for 1/4 cup of cinnamon.

2 7-1/2 oz. tubes refrigerated
   biscuits, quartered
1/2 c. butter, melted
1/4 c. cinnamon

1/2 c. sugar
Optional: additional melted
   butter

Roll biscuit quarters into balls; set aside. Place melted butter in a shallow bowl; blend cinnamon and sugar in a separate bowl. Roll dough balls in melted butter, then in cinnamon-sugar. Spray a 9" round cake pan with non-stick vegetable spray. Arrange coated balls in pan, sides touching. Drizzle with any remaining butter; melt a little more butter if too little is left. Sprinkle with any remaining cinnamon-sugar. Bake at 400 degrees for 15 to 20 minutes, until golden. Cool slightly before serving. Serves 6.

Fast French Toast

Kathy Courington
Canton, GA

We love breakfast for dinner! When we are in a hurry, this fits
the bill. Just add some fresh fruit and you're in business.

2 eggs, beaten	1/8 t. salt
1 c. milk	8 slices bread
1/4 t. cinnamon	Garnish: butter, warmed
1/8 t. nutmeg	pancake syrup

In a shallow bowl, whisk together eggs, milk, spices and salt; set aside.
Dip each slice of bread into egg mixture, coating both sides. Heat a
skillet over medium heat; spray with non-stick vegetable spray, if not
using a non-stick skillet. Working in batches, add bread slices to skillet;
cook until golden on both sides. Serve with butter and warmed syrup.
Serves 4, 2 slices each.

Whip up a crock of marmalade butter...delicious on hot toast,
waffles and more. Simply blend together one cup softened
butter, 1/2 cup honey and 1/4 cup orange marmalade.

COZY HOLIDAY
Breakfasts

Easy Banana Pancakes

Kathy Grashoff
Fort Wayne, IN

This is a "sit down and take your time" kind of breakfast. These pancakes go together quick as a wink, and they're scrumptious. For a change from maple syrup, try strawberry jam...yummy!

2 c. biscuit baking mix
1 c. milk
2 eggs, lightly beaten

2 ripe bananas, mashed
Garnish: butter, maple syrup

In a large bowl, combine biscuit mix, milk, eggs and bananas, stirring just until moistened. Pour 1/4 cup batter per pancake onto a hot, lightly greased griddle. Cook until edges look done and bubbles form on top; turn and cook other side. Serve immediately, garnished as desired. Makes 16 pancakes.

Whip up some snowman pancakes, just for fun! Simply arrange 2 or 3 pancakes to form a snowman. Add chocolate chip eyes and buttons and a strip of crispy bacon for a scarf. The kids will love it!

Chorizo Mexican Quiche

Rosalie Zarybnicky
Boise, ID

This quiche is the perfect dish to serve for a family brunch with pastries and fresh fruits. We have served it at many of our Christmas brunches. Since the recipe makes two quiches, it's perfect for potlucks too.

2 9-inch pie crusts, unbaked
12-oz. chorizo pork sausage
  link, casing removed
1-1/2 c. shredded Monterey Jack
  cheese
8-oz. container sour cream
4 eggs, beaten
4-oz. can diced green chiles

3-1/4 oz. can sliced black olives,
  drained
1/2 c. green taco sauce
1/4 c. green onions, chopped
1/4 t. ground cumin
Optional: 1/8 t. hot pepper
  seasoning

Bake pie crusts at 350 degrees for 10 minutes; set aside to cool. Meanwhile, brown sausage in a large skillet over medium heat; drain. Stir in remaining ingredients. Divide sausage mixture between baked pie crusts. Bake at 350 degrees for 35 to 40 minutes. Makes 2 quiches; each serves 6.

Make a quick, savory crumb crust for a quiche. Spread 2-1/2 tablespoons softened butter in a pie plate, then firmly press 2-1/2 cups crushed tortilla chips or cracker crumbs into the butter. Freeze until firm, pour in filling and bake as directed.

Mixed-Up Ham & Egg Muffins

Amy Thomason Hunt
Traphill, NC

These tasty muffins are perfect for brunch alongside a fruit salad.

1 doz. eggs, beaten
1/2 c. onion, diced
1/4 c. green pepper, chopped
1/2 c. mushrooms, chopped
1/4 t. garlic powder

1/2 t. salt
1/4 t. pepper
1/2 lb. cooked ham, diced
1/2 c. shredded Cheddar cheese

In a large bowl, whisk together eggs, vegetables and seasonings. Stir in ham and cheese. Spray 12 muffin cups with non-stick vegetable spray. Spoon egg mixture into muffin cups, filling 1/3 full. Bake at 350 degrees for 20 to 25 minutes. Makes one dozen.

Pot of Gold Punch

Suzanne Stroud
Bremen, GA

My mom made this punch every Christmas, and I have carried on the tradition for my family. It's a wonderful beverage for Christmas morning breakfast. We find ourselves coming up with lots of other times to enjoy it!

6 c. pineapple juice, chilled
4 c. orange juice, chilled

6 c. ginger ale, chilled

Combine all ingredients in a one-gallon pitcher; stir gently and serve immediately. If preferred, add ginger ale at serving time; stir again. Makes 16 servings, one cup each.

Keep punch from becoming diluted. Just freeze cranberry or pineapple juice in an angel food cake pan. Pop it out and add to the punch bowl.

Overnight Ham & Cheddar Baked Egg Casserole

Judy Loemker
Edwardsville, IL

This flavorful recipe received rave reviews from our guests as they joined us for brunch one day many years ago. But don't wait for special guests to visit...your family will love this one too! Feel free to omit any vegetables that aren't to your family's liking. It would also be delicious with chopped tomatoes, fresh basil and extra cheese sprinkled on top just before serving.

1 onion, chopped
2 to 3 t. butter
6 slices whole-wheat or multi-grain bread
2 c. cooked ham, diced
1-1/2 c. fresh spinach, chopped
3/4 c. red pepper, chopped
3/4 c. black olives, chopped
1 c. sliced mushrooms

8-oz. pkg. shredded Cheddar cheese
4-1/2 oz. can chopped green chiles
8 eggs, beaten
3 c. milk
1 t. dry mustard
1/2 t. pepper
Optional: 1 t. dried oregano

In a skillet over medium heat, sauté onion in butter; cool. Meanwhile, spray a 13"x9" baking pan with non-stick vegetable spray. Line the bottom of pan with bread slices. Layer with ham, spinach, red pepper, olives, mushrooms and onion. Sprinkle cheese and chiles on top; set aside. Whisk together eggs, milk and seasonings in a large bowl; pour over mixture in pan. Cover and refrigerate overnight. Bake, uncovered, at 350 degrees for one hour, or until top is golden and center tests done. Serves 8.

Cheese toast is delicious alongside savory breakfast dishes...and a snap to make on a countertop grill. Spread softened butter over slices of French bread and grill until golden, then sprinkle with your favorite cheese.

Breakfasts

Banana-Walnut Coffee Cake

Sandra Mirando
Depew, NY

This cake is so good that we look forward to having overripe bananas so we can make it. It tastes even better the next day or so...but doesn't stay around long!

2 eggs, beaten
1/2 c. shortening
1-1/2 c. sugar
3 ripe bananas, mashed
1 t. vanilla extract
1 t. baking soda
1/4 c. buttermilk

1-1/2 c. all-purpose flour
3/4 t. salt
1 c. chopped walnuts
1 c. brown sugar, packed
1/2 c. butter
1 c. sweetened flaked coconut

In a large bowl, stir together eggs, shortening, sugar, bananas and vanilla until well blended; set aside. Dissolve baking soda in buttermilk; add to egg mixture and stir well. Add flour and salt; mix well. Fold in walnuts. Pour batter into a greased and floured 13"x9" baking pan; set aside. In a saucepan, combine brown sugar, butter and coconut. Cook over low heat, stirring constantly, until butter melts. Spoon brown sugar mixture over batter. Bake at 350 degrees for 45 minutes, or until a toothpick comes out clean. Makes 15 servings.

Grandma's well-loved cookie cutters hold too many happy memories to be hidden in a drawer. Tie them to a grapevine wreath and add a big gingham bow for a delightful kitchen decoration.

Simple Baked Oatmeal

Coleen Lambert
Luxemburg, WI

*Top with some Wisconsin maple syrup and it'll really
hit the spot on a cold day. So good!*

4 eggs, beaten
3-1/3 c. milk
1 T. oil
1 T. vanilla extract
1 t. cinnamon
1/2 t. salt
3/4 c. brown sugar, packed

2-1/4 c. quick-cooking oats,
  uncooked
Optional: 3/4 c. dried fruit,
  chopped
Garnish: maple syrup and milk
  or cream

In a bowl, whisk together eggs, milk, oil, vanilla, cinnamon and salt.
Stir in brown sugar, oats and fruit, if using. Transfer to a greased
8"x8" baking pan. Bake, uncovered, at 350 degrees for 55 to
60 minutes. Serve topped with maple syrup and milk or cream.
Serves 6.

Breakfast with Santa! Ask a family friend to play Santa for
the children at your holiday brunch. They'll love sharing
secrets with the jolly old elf over waffles and hot cocoa.

Spiced Orange Tea

Jennifer Niemi
Nova Scotia, Canada

I love to make this hot drink in the wintertime! After shoveling or taking a long walk in the cold air, there's nothing more warming than an afternoon spent sipping this tea while curled up with a good book. It could make you love wintertime!

12 c. cold water, divided
zest of 1 large orange
5 6-inch cinnamon sticks
2-1/4 t. whole cloves
1 t. whole allspice

1 c. powdered sweetened
  iced tea mix
1/2 c. powdered sweetened
  orange drink mix

In a small saucepan, combine 2 cups water, orange zest and spices. Bring to a boil over high heat; reduce heat to medium-low. Cover and simmer for 20 minutes. Strain, discarding zest and spices; add reserved liquid to a large saucepan. Stir in remaining water and drink mixes. Cook over low heat, stirring often, until drink mixes have dissolved. Increase heat to medium-high; heat until piping hot. Makes 12 servings.

Give mugs for winter beverages...oh-so-easy! Grocery stores, drugstores and even tag sales all have fun mugs to choose from. Fill them full of packets of hot cocoa, coffee or tea bags. Tie up mugs in squares of tulle and add a card that says "Thinking warm thoughts of you."

Bacon Breakfast Casserole

Arlene Crouse
North Lima, OH

When my grandchildren were still living at home, I would make this breakfast dish on Christmas Eve. Then on Christmas Day, it was popped into the oven to bake while they opened their presents. Make some toast, pour the orange juice...breakfast is served!

6 slices bread, cubed
1 lb. bacon, diced and crisply
   cooked
1 c. shredded Cheddar cheese

6 eggs, beaten
2 c. milk
1 t. dry mustard
1 t. Worcestershire sauce

Spread bread cubes in a greased 13"x9" baking pan. Top with bacon and cheese; set aside. In a large bowl, whisk together remaining ingredients; pour over top. Cover and refrigerate overnight. Uncover and bake at 350 degrees for 50 to 60 minutes, until set and golden. Makes 8 to 10 servings.

Cannons' 5-Minute Cocoa

Iris Cannon
Buda, TX

My grandmother gave me this recipe when I was 13.
Now I make it for my three girls, and they love it too.

6 c. water
6 T. baking cocoa
1/4 t. salt
1 t. vanilla extract

14-oz. can sweetened condensed
   milk
Optional: 1 T. instant coffee
   granules

Heat water in a saucepan over medium heat. Add cocoa and mix completely; stir in salt. Heat until steaming, but do not let boil. Add vanilla. Pour in condensed milk while stirring to prevent scorching. Add instant coffee, if using; stir to dissolve. Heat through. If too warm, allow to cool slightly before serving. Serves 6 to 8.

Christmas is the family time,
the good time of the year.

–Samuel Johnson

MAKING
MERRY
Together

5-Layer Italian Dip

Vicki Nelson
Puyallup, WA

This dip is gone in no time! I can't tell you how many times I have shared this recipe. With the red and green colors used, it's especially nice around the holidays. If I take it to a potluck and the oven is being used, I just pop it in the microwave for about 5 minutes, and it turns out just as well. I like to use a quiche dish for a pretty presentation.

8-oz. container whipped
    cream cheese
1/4 c. grated Parmesan cheese
1/3 c. basil pesto sauce
1/2 c. roasted red peppers,
    drained and chopped

1 c. shredded mozzarella
    cheese
snack crackers or sliced
    Italian bread

In a bowl, blend together cream cheese and Parmesan cheese. Spread in the bottom of a 9" quiche dish or pie plate. Spread pesto sauce over cheese mixture. Sprinkle red peppers over pesto sauce. Sprinkle mozzarella cheese over the peppers. Bake, uncovered, at 350 degrees for 15 minutes, or until heated through and cheeses are melted. Serve hot with crackers or Italian bread. Serves 8.

Whether it's a holiday open house, a tree trimming party or a family get-together, appetizer parties are a great way to visit with friends during the busy holiday season. The recipes are so quick & easy to prepare...more time can be spent having fun together.

Pine Cone Cheese Ball

Diana Lamphere
Colorado Springs, CO

A basic cheese ball, but very good. It's pretty served on a faux pine bough...takes a little time to arrange the almonds, but it's worth it. Rave reviews! You can also decorate it in many other ways. Roll it in chopped walnuts or pecans, or make it into a snowman.

1-1/2 c. cream cheese, softened	1/2 t. dried oregano
1/2 c. grated Parmesan cheese	1/8 t. garlic salt, or to taste
1/4 c. mayonnaise	6-oz. pkg. sliced almonds

In a large bowl, combine all ingredients except almonds; blend well. Shape into a large egg shape; place on a serving plate. Layer with sliced almonds in rows to resemble a pine cone. Cover and refrigerate until serving time. Makes one large cheese ball.

Craft a fun snowball wreath that won't melt! Hot-glue
fuzzy white pompoms over a foam wreath,
then top it with a simple bow.

Mushroom-Bacon Roll-Ups

Beverlee Traxler
British Columbia, Canada

*These tasty tidbits are popular at Christmas! They freeze very well,
so they're handy for guests on a moment's notice.*

1/2 lb. bacon, coarsely chopped
2 onions, finely chopped
2/3 lb. mushrooms, finely
   chopped
1 t. Dijon mustard

8-oz. pkg. cream cheese, room
   temperature
20 slices bread, crusts trimmed
1/4 c. butter, melted

In a skillet over medium heat, cook bacon for about 5 minutes. Add
onions and mushrooms. Cook, stirring often, until softened, about
5 minutes; drain. Stir in mustard and cream cheese; remove from heat.
Flatten bread slices gently with a rolling pin. Spread 2 tablespoons
bacon mixture over each slice. Roll bread slices into small logs; slice
each log in half. Place roll-ups seam-side down on an ungreased
baking sheet; brush lightly with melted butter. Bake on center rack at
375 degrees until golden, about 15 minutes. May also freeze baked
roll-ups on baking sheet; store in a freezer container until ready to
serve. Remove desired number to a baking sheet; bake at 400 degrees
for 12 to 15 minutes. Makes about 3-1/2 dozen.

Serve easy-to-handle foods and beverages at tables in
several different rooms around the house. Guests will
be able to snack and mingle easily.

Smoky Chicken Spread

Vickie
Gooseberry Patch

This savory, crunchy spread is always a hit at parties.

3 c. cooked chicken, finely
  chopped
1/2 c. celery, finely chopped
1/2 c. smoked almonds, coarsely
  chopped
1/4 c. onion, finely chopped

3/4 c. mayonnaise
1 T. honey
1/2 t. seasoned salt
1/8 t. pepper
assorted snack crackers

In a bowl, combine all ingredients except crackers; mix well. Cover and chill at least 2 hours before serving. Serve with snack crackers. Serves 10 to 12.

Welcome guests with a line of Mason jar luminarias along your front walk. Simply fill jars half full with rock salt and nestle tea lights in the salt. The flames will make the salt sparkle like ice crystals.

Centralia Cheese Ball

Andrea Heyart
Savannah, TX

My dad used to make these cheese balls every Christmas for the local grocery store in the small town of Centralia, Illinois. He continued to make them for our family every Christmas for years. Now I continue the tradition and make Dad's cheese ball for Christmas.

1-1/2 lbs. Cheddar cheese, diced
1 lb. Colby Jack cheese, diced
1/2 lb. Swiss cheese, diced
4-oz. pkg. crumbled blue cheese
20-oz. jar mayonnaise
4-1/2 T. Worcestershire sauce

3-1/2 t. chili powder
1 T. garlic powder
1-1/2 T. caraway seed
1 T. salt
1 t. dry mustard
Garnish: paprika to taste

Combine cheeses in a large bowl; mix together and set aside. In a separate bowl, stir together mayonnaise and Worcestershire sauce; fold into cheese mixture. Combine all seasonings in another bowl; stir into cheese mixture. Working in batches, process cheese mixture in a food grinder or food mill. Form into 2 to 3 balls. Sprinkle tops with paprika. Wrap individually in plastic wrap; chill. Makes 2 to 3 cheese balls; each ball serves 6 to 8.

Have an appetizer swap with 3 or 4 girlfriends! Each makes a big batch of her favorite dip, spread or finger food, then you all get together to sample and divide 'em up. You'll all have a super variety of goodies for holiday parties.

Slow-Cooker Holiday Wassail

Tiffany Jones
Locust Grove, AR

When I was growing up, I became familiar with this wonderful warm comforting beverage. My brother Darrin always wanted Mom to fix this during the holidays.

48-oz. can pineapple juice
48-oz. can orange juice
2-ltr. bottle ginger ale
7.4-oz. pkg. spiced apple
   cider mix

3 4-inch cinnamon sticks
2 whole cloves

Combine juices and ginger ale in a 6-quart slow cooker. Add all packets of cider mix; stir well. Cover and cook on high setting for 2 hours, or on low setting for 4 hours. Discard whole spices before serving. Makes 10 servings.

Fizzy Evergreen Bowl

Carolyn Deckard
Bedford, IN

We all love this simple punch! We serve it often at Christmas and other times too. Everyone will be waiting in line for this punch.

4 pts. lime sherbet,
   divided

1-ltr. bottle lemon-lime
   soda, chilled

Spoon 3 pints of sherbet into a punch bowl; let soften at room temperature for about 5 minutes. Slowly pour in chilled soda, stirring slightly to combine with sherbet. Float generous scoops of remaining sherbet on top. Makes 36 punch cup servings.

Dress up the beverage station at your holiday buffet. Fasten a festive ribbon around a punch bowl and set it in a fresh pine wreath...so pretty!

Cheese & Spinach Puffs

Leona Krivda
Belle Vernon, PA

I love to make easy-to-freeze treats like this around the holidays!
With five or six different appetizers tucked in the freezer,
you always have a nice assortment for guests.

10-oz. pkg. frozen chopped
  spinach
1/2 c. onion, finely minced
1/2 c. shredded Cheddar cheese
1/2 c. shredded Parmesan
  cheese

1/2 c. blue cheese salad dressing
2 eggs, beaten
1/4 c. margarine, melted and
  cooled slightly
1/8 t. garlic powder
8-1/2 oz. pkg. corn muffin mix

Cook spinach according to package directions, adding onion as it
cooks. Drain spinach very well, squeezing out all excess liquid.
Meanwhile, in a bowl, combine remaining ingredients except corn
muffin mix; stir well. Add spinach mixture and muffin mix; stir very
well. Cover and chill for 2 hours. Roll mixture into one-inch balls;
arrange on an ungreased baking sheet. Bake at 350 degrees for
12 to 15 minutes, until hot and cheese is melted. Serve warm. May
also freeze unbaked balls in a freezer container until ready to serve.
Remove desired number to a baking sheet; bake as above. Makes
5 dozen.

The secret to being a relaxed hostess...choose foods like
Cheese & Spinach Puffs that can be prepared in advance.
At party time, simply pull from the fridge and serve,
or pop into a hot oven as needed.

Green Chile Sourdough Bites

Naomi Townsend
Ozark, MO

We like to serve these tasty appetizers when our car club friends gather after a car show. I like to use small loaves of sourdough bread, sliced with an electric knife.

4-oz. can diced mild green chiles
1/2 c. butter, room temperature
1/2 c. mayonnaise
8-oz. pkg. shredded Monterey
   Jack cheese

1 loaf sourdough bread,
   cut into small bites
garlic powder to taste

In a bowl, mix chiles, butter and mayonnaise until smooth. Add cheese and stir to combine. Mixture may now be covered and refrigerated for later use. Spread chile mixture onto bread pieces. Arrange in a single layer on an aluminum foil-lined baking sheet. Sprinkle with garlic powder. Bake at 450 degrees until bubbly and crisp, about 3 to 4 minutes. Serves 12.

Use tiered cake stands for bite-size appetizers...so handy, and they take up less space on the buffet table than setting out several serving platters.

Meatballs for a Crowd

Sheri Dulaney
Englewood, OH

I came up with this recipe to take to a family Christmas gathering.
Everyone really liked them...the bowl was empty when it was time
to go home! You can enjoy some now, and freeze some for later.

1 lb. ground beef
1/2 c. rolled oats, uncooked
2/3 c. milk
2 t. dried, minced onion
1 t. salt
1/2 t. pepper

1 c. all-purpose flour
2 T. oil
3/4 c. catsup
6 T. brown sugar, packed
3/4 t. Worcestershire sauce

In a large bowl, combine uncooked beef, oats, milk, onion and
seasonings. Mix well; form into 1-1/2 inch balls. Roll lightly in flour;
set aside. Heat oil in a skillet over medium heat; add meatballs. Cook
until browned lightly on all sides. Combine remaining ingredients in
a small bowl; add to hot meatballs in skillet. Cook and stir over
medium-low heat until sauce is warmed through. Makes 1-1/2 to
2 dozen.

Set the mood with jolly Christmas music! Ask guests
to bring along their favorites for a festive variety
all evening long.

MAKING MERRY
Together

Buffalo Ranch Meatballs

*Jill Ball
Highland, UT*

*On Christmas Eve, our family's fun tradition is gathering
around the tree laughing, talking and eating appetizers.
We serve up lots of little goodies like these meatballs.*

26-oz. pkg. frozen meatballs
12-oz. hot wing buffalo sauce

1-oz. pkg. ranch salad
dressing mix

Add frozen meatballs to a 4-quart slow cooker; set aside. Combine
sauce and dressing mix in a bowl; stir well and pour over meatballs.
Cover and cook on high setting for 2 hours, or on low setting for
4 hours, stirring occasionally. Serves 10 to 12.

A veggie-packed Christmas tree will certainly "spruce" up
your buffet table! Cover a tall styrofoam cone with aluminum
foil. Attach broccoli flowerets and cherry tomatoes by
sticking one end of a toothpick into the veggie and the
other end into the cone. Serve with a yummy veggie dip.

Holly Jolly Party Mix

Mary Little
Franklin, TN

This is a recipe that I make for the holiday season. It is quick & easy and always a hit with my family. You can vary the ingredients to suit your family's taste. A container of this mix makes a nice gift.

6 c. bite-size crispy rice cereal squares
6 c. bite-size crispy corn cereal squares
10-oz. pkg. oyster crackers
8-oz. pkg. mini pretzels
1 c. cashews or other nuts
3/4 c. canola oil
2-oz. pkg. ranch salad dressing mix

Combine cereals, crackers, pretzels and nuts in a clean brown paper grocery bag. Shake to mix; set aside. Combine oil and ranch dressing in a bowl. Stir well; drizzle over cereal mixture. Let stand for 2 hours, shaking bag occasionally. Store in an airtight container. Makes about 25 cups.

I wish we could put up some of the Christmas spirit
in jars and open a jar of it every month.

–Harlan Miller

Together

Spicy Pretzel Sticks

Pat Palamar
Las Vegas, NV

My family loves to munch on these zesty pretzels! Increase the amount of cayenne pepper for those who like it really spicy. You can even omit the cayenne...the pretzels will still be very tasty.

12-oz. pkg. pretzel sticks
1/2 c. oil
1-oz. pkg. ranch salad
   dressing mix

1 t. garlic salt
1 t. cayenne pepper,
   or to taste

Spread pretzel sticks on an ungreased baking sheet in a single layer; set aside. Combine remaining ingredients in a bowl; mix well. Drizzle oil mixture evenly over pretzels. Bake at 250 degrees for about one hour. Cool; store loosely covered. Makes 12 servings.

Dill Ranch Crackers

Sheri Haney
Winchester, IN

I received some of these crackers as a gift one year, and I make them every Christmas to give to my beauty salon customers. One of my favorite ways to eat them is to toss a handful into a bowl of tomato soup...yum!

2 12-oz. pkg. oyster crackers
12-oz. pkg. baked cheese snack
   crackers
3 to 4 c. pretzel sticks
16-oz. bottle butter-flavored
   popcorn oil

1-oz. pkg. ranch salad
   dressing mix
2 T. dill weed

Combine crackers and pretzels in a large bowl; toss to mix and set aside. In a separate bowl, combine oil, dressing mix and dill weed; mix well. Drizzle oil mixture over cracker mixture; stir well. Cover and let stand for one day before serving. Flip container occasionally until oil is completely absorbed. Makes 12 servings.

Paper muffin cup liners come in all colors...great for serving individual portions of party mix.

Christmas Cheese Ball

Kathy Gideon
Contort, TN

My mother-in-law used to make a delicious cheese ball every year at Christmas. She is no longer with us, and I never did get her recipe. So, I experimented, knowing some of her ingredients, until I believe I have it! Now, I make this every year for my family at Christmas, and we love it.

2 8-oz. pkg. cream cheese,
    softened
8-oz. pkg. finely shredded mild
    Cheddar cheese
1 T. chopped pimentos, drained
1 T. onion, finely chopped
1 T. green pepper, finely
    chopped

2 T. Worcestershire sauce
1 T. lemon juice
1/4 to 1/2 t. garlic salt,
    to taste
1/2 c. chopped pecans
assorted crackers

In a large bowl, combine all ingredients except pecans and crackers. Mix thoroughly and shape into a ball. Roll in pecans to coat. Wrap in plastic wrap and chill well. Serve with assorted crackers. Makes about 3 cups.

Creamy dips and spreads are twice as tasty with homemade baguette crisps. Thinly slice a French loaf on the diagonal and arrange slices on a baking sheet. Sprinkle with olive oil and garlic powder, then bake at 400 degrees for 12 to 15 minutes.

Pull-Apart Bacon & Cheese Bread

Brittney Swartzendruber
John Day, OR

So easy and fun to make! I let my children help.

12 slices bacon, diced
16-oz. loaf frozen bread
   dough, thawed
2 T. olive oil, divided

1 c. shredded mozzarella
   cheese
1-oz. pkg. ranch salad
   dressing mix

In a skillet over medium heat, cook bacon for 5 minutes, or until partially cooked. Drain bacon on paper towels. Meanwhile, roll out dough to 1/2-inch thickness; brush with one tablespoon oil. Cut dough into one-inch cubes; place in a large bowl. Add bacon, cheese, dressing mix and remaining oil; toss to coat. Arrange dough pieces on a greased baking sheet in a 9-inch by 5-inch oval, layering as needed. Cover with a tea towel; let rise in a warm place for 30 minutes. Bake at 350 degrees for 15 minutes. Cover with aluminum foil. Bake 5 to 10 minutes longer, until golden. Serves 12 to 16.

For a sparkly centerpiece in a jiffy, arrange shiny ornament
balls in a glass bowl. Wind shining silver garland
through the ornaments...beautiful!

Greek Pinwheels

Leona Krivda
Belle Vernon, PA

These delicious appetizers are a little different, and they've always been well liked by everyone. I love feta cheese, and these have just the right amount. Enjoy!

1 T. egg, beaten
3/4 t. water
1 sheet frozen puff pastry, thawed
1/3 c. marinated quartered artichoke hearts, very well drained

1 T. oil-packed sun-dried tomatoes, very well drained
3 Greek olives, very well drained
1/2 c. cream cheese, softened
1/4 c. crumbled feta cheese
1 t. Greek seasoning

Whisk together egg and water in a cup. Unfold puff pastry; brush with egg mixture and set aside. Finely chop artichokes, tomatoes and olives and add to a bowl. Blend in cheeses and seasoning. Spread mixture over pastry to within 1/2-inch of edges. Roll up jelly-roll style, starting on one long edge. Cut into 20 slices, each 1/2-inch thick. Place pinwheels on a greased baking sheet, 2 inches apart. Bake at 425 degrees for 9 to 11 minutes, until puffed and golden. Serve warm. Makes 20 pieces.

Make a party tray of savory appetizer tarts...guests will never guess how easy it is! Bake frozen mini phyllo shells according to package directions, then spoon in a favorite savory dip or spread.

Italian Chicken Wings

Peggy Lopes
Cranston, RI

These crisp, yummy wings are a family favorite at birthday parties, football gatherings and the Fourth of July.

1/2 c. low-calorie Italian salad dressing
4 0.7-oz. pkgs. Italian salad dressing mix

5 lbs. chicken wings, separated

In a large bowl, mix together salad dressing and dressing mix to make a paste. Place chicken wings on a lightly greased baking sheet; brush with paste. Bake at 400 degrees for 60 minutes, turning occasionally, or until wings are crisp and golden. Serves 6 to 8.

For an elegant yet oh-so-easy appetizer, try a cheese platter. Choose a soft cheese, a hard cheese and a semi-soft or crumbly cheese. Add a basket of crisp crackers, crusty baguette slices and some sliced apples or pears. So simple, yet sure to please guests!

Roasted Tomato Bruschetta

Danyel Martin
Madisonville, KY

This colorful dish is a favorite in our Italian household,
no matter what the season. It's delicious as an appetizer
or served with a pasta dish.

3 pts. cherry tomatoes
1-1/2 T. olive oil
3 cloves minced garlic
1/8 t. salt, or to taste
1/2 t. pepper

1 t. red wine vinegar
1/2 c. fresh basil, sliced and
 divided
12 to 14 slices baguette,
 toasted

In a large bowl, toss tomatoes with oil, garlic, salt and pepper. Spread
on an ungreased baking sheet. Bake at 325 degrees for 45 to
50 minutes, until tomatoes are softened and broken down. Remove
tomato mixture to a bowl. Add vinegar and 1/4 cup basil; toss to mix.
At serving time, spoon tomato mixture onto baguette slices; garnish
with remaining basil. Makes 12 to 14 pieces.

Turn your favorite shredded pork or beef into party food...
serve up bite-size portions on slider buns. Guests will
love sampling a little of everything.

Olive Tapenade

Joan Chance
Houston, TX

For anyone who loves olives! Serve with toast points,
crisp toasted breads or assorted crackers.

3 c. green and black olives,
   pitted, drained and rinsed
1 anchovy fillet, rinsed, or
   1 t. anchovy paste

2 t. garlic, minced
1 T. capers, drained
1 T. fresh lemon juice
2 T. olive oil

Add all ingredients to a food processor. Process for one to 2 minutes, scraping down sides of bowl, until coarsely chopped or to the texture of a spread. Makes 16 servings.

Parmesan-Stuffed Mushrooms

Bobbie Metzger
Pittsburgh, PA

This recipe was given to me years ago by a wonderful cook. It's the
first thing I think of whenever I'm asked to a special occasion.

8-oz. pkg. cream cheese,
   softened
1 c. grated Parmesan cheese
1/2 t. garlic salt

1/4 c. whipping cream
24 large mushrooms, stems
   removed
1/2 c. butter, melted

In a bowl, blend cheeses and garlic salt; slowly stir in cream. Spoon cheese mixture into mushroom. Dip bottoms of mushroom caps into melted butter; place on an ungreased baking sheet. Bake at 350 degrees for 15 minutes, or until tops are lightly golden. Makes 2 dozen.

When making stuffed mushrooms, don't discard the stems! Chop and sauté them for a delicious addition to scrambled eggs.

Party Ham Sandwiches

Marla Kinnersley
Surprise, AZ

This is my version of those baked ham sandwiches that everyone just loves. Whenever I serve them, I'm asked for the recipe. They're amazingly flavorful...they'll become a favorite of yours too!

12 Hawaiian sweet rolls
8-oz. container spreadable chive
  & onion cream cheese
1/2 lb. thinly sliced deli Black
  Forest ham
1/2 lb. sliced Swiss cheese

1/4 c. butter, melted
1/4 c. grated Parmesan cheese
1 T. Worcestershire sauce
2-1/4 t. mustard
1-1/2 t. poppy seed
1-1/2 t. dried, minced onion

Slice open the rolls; place the bottom rolls in a greased 13"x9" baking pan. Spread cream cheese over rolls; layer with ham and cheese slices. Add roll tops; set aside. Combine remaining ingredients in a small bowl; drizzle over rolls. Cover with aluminum foil. Bake at 350 degrees for 20 minutes, or until cheese is melted, watching closely so rolls don't burn on the bottom. Makes one dozen.

Short on time? Keep party time super-simple. Serve one or 2 tried & true appetizers like cheese balls and dips, and pick up some tasty go-withs like pickles, marinated olives and cocktail nuts at the grocery store. Relax and enjoy your guests!

Tater-Dipped Veggies

Mary Lou Savage
McKeesport, PA

On a cool evening, this recipe is a favorite to snack on as our family watches a football game or a favorite movie.

1 c. instant mashed potato
    flakes
1/3 c. grated Parmesan cheese
1/4 c. butter, melted and cooled
1/2 t. celery salt
1/4 t. garlic powder
2 eggs

4 to 5 c. assorted fresh
    vegetables (mushrooms,
    peppers, cauliflower,
    broccoli, zucchini and
    steamed carrots), cut into
    bite-size pieces
Garnish: ranch salad dressing

In a shallow bowl, combine potato flakes, Parmesan cheese, melted butter and seasonings. Beat eggs in another shallow bowl. Dip vegetables, one at a time, into egg then into potato mixture, coating well. Arrange vegetables on a lightly greased baking sheet. Bake at 400 degrees for 20 to 25 minutes, until tender. Serve warm with ranch dressing. Makes 6 to 8 servings.

Love candlelight at Christmas, but you're concerned about children and pets knocking over lit candles? Tuck battery-operated tealights and pillars into favorite votives, sconces and centerpieces for a safe, soft glow.

Salmon Cheese Ball

Danielle Stenger
Orchard, CO

Our whole family has a large Christmas Eve get-together every year, and I always make this cheese ball for it. Even the kids love it!

14-3/4 oz. can salmon, drained
8-oz. pkg. cream cheese,
   softened
1 T. smoke-flavored cooking
   sauce

3/4 c. onion, diced
dried parsley to taste
assorted crackers

Pick through salmon, discarding any bones. Transfer to a large bowl and flake with a fork. Add cream cheese, sauce and onion; blend well. Lay out a piece of plastic wrap; sprinkle parsley generously all over plastic wrap. Spoon salmon mixture out onto plastic wrap. Gather plastic wrap around mixture; place into a bowl. Wrap mixture tightly; form to the bowl. Refrigerate for at least one hour. Lift cheese ball out of bowl; unwrap onto a serving plate and surround with assorted crackers. Serves 10.

Invert a glass garden cloche and fill it with shiny Christmas ornaments, then cover with a plate and turn it right-side up...beautiful!

Spicy Seafood Dip

Mary Beth Bosco
Camillus, NY

I have made this dip for many occasions...holidays, football tailgating parties, wine nights with the girls. Sometimes I'll change out the seafood I use, but it's delicious as is.

8-oz. pkg. cream cheese, softened
1/4 c. chili sauce
1/4 to 1/2 t. hot pepper sauce
1 t. lemon juice
1 c. cooked shrimp, crabmeat or clams, chopped

4 green onions, sliced, including some tops
1/4 c. red pepper, finely chopped
1/4 c. celery, finely chopped
snack crackers, bagel chips or pita crisps

In a bowl, combine cream cheese, sauces and lemon juice. Stir in seafood, onions, pepper and celery. Cover and chill until serving time. Serve with crackers, bagel chips or pita crisps. Serves 8.

A guideline for appetizers...allow 6 to 8 servings per person if dinner will follow. Plan for 12 to 15 per person if it's an appetizer-only gathering.

'Tis The Season Taco Dip

Amy Thomason Hunt
Traphill, NC

I always make this tasty dip for family gatherings, holidays and just whenever the munchies hit. It's especially pretty at Christmastime with the red and green colors of the veggies on top.

2 15-oz. cans refried beans
1-1/4 oz. pkg. taco seasoning
   mix
4-oz. can chopped green chiles
16-oz. container sour cream
8-oz. pkg. shredded Mexican
   blend cheese

4-oz. can chopped black olives,
   drained
1 tomato, diced
4 to 5 green onions, diced
tortilla chips

Mix refried beans and taco seasoning together. Spread in a lightly greased 2-quart casserole dish. Spread chiles over bean mixture; layer with sour cream, cheese and vegetables. Cover and chill until serving time. Serve with tortilla chips. Makes 10 to 12 servings.

1-2-3 Pizza Dip

Cyndy DeStefano
Hermitage, PA

This is a quick & easy dish to take to a last-minute get-together. Everyone loves it, and it's a snap to make.

8-oz. pkg. cream cheese,
   softened
15-oz. jar pizza sauce
3-1/2 oz. pkg. sliced pepperoni

8-oz. pkg. shredded mozzarella
   cheese
tortilla chips

Spread cream cheese evenly in a 9" glass pie plate. Top with pizza sauce, pepperoni and shredded cheese. Microwave, uncovered, on high for one minute, or until bubbly and cheese is melted. Serve with tortilla chips. Serves 10 to 12.

Make notes all year 'round...at Christmastime, you'll know just what to get everyone!

Together

Mexican Phyllo Bites

Barbara Topp
Holly Springs, NC

*My family's most-requested appetizer! It's a must at all holiday
celebrations. The filling can be made ahead and frozen,
then just thaw when ready to serve.*

10-oz. can diced tomatoes and
   green chiles, drained
3-oz. pkg. real bacon bits
1 c. mayonnaise

1-1/2 c. shredded Colby-Jack
   cheese
3 2-oz. pkgs. frozen mini phyllo
   shells

In a bowl, mix together tomatoes, bacon bits and mayonnaise. Add
cheese; stir until blended. Spoon mixture into phyllo shells; arrange on
an ungreased baking sheet. Bake at 350 degrees for 15 to 20 minutes,
until golden and cheese is melted. Makes about 4 dozen.

Beefy Bean Dip

Chrissy Ludwig
Columbus, OH

*I've made this for my family since 1988. We just call it "The Dip"
and everyone loves it. It's great for a party or a potluck dinner! It is
very quick & easy to prepare. Serve with tortilla chips or scoop-type
corn chips.*

1 lb. ground beef chuck
16-oz. can traditional refried
   beans
4-oz. can fire-roasted diced
   mild green chiles

16-oz. jar mild traditional salsa
8-oz. pkg. finely shredded Colby
   Jack cheese

Brown beef in a skillet over medium heat; drain. Transfer to a
13" covered oval roasting pan. Add beans, chiles, salsa and cheese;
mix gently. Cover pan with lid. Bake at 350 degrees for 30 to
40 minutes, until slightly bubbly and cheese is melted. Serve in bowls
with tortilla chips on the side. Leftovers reheat well in a microwave
oven. Serves 6 to 8.

Small cheer and great welcome make a merry feast!
–William Shakespeare

Mint Chocolate Chip-Peppermint Cheese Ball

Kim Turechek
Oklahoma City, OK

This is a great "trim the tree" appetizer! Or place it in a napkin-lined basket and add some cookies...a beautiful gift to give to office co-workers.

8-oz. pkg. cream cheese, softened
1/2 c. butter, softened
1/2 t. peppermint extract
3/4 c. powdered sugar

1-1/2 c. mint chocolate chips
1/2 c. peppermint candy, crushed
graham cracker snack sticks or thin mint wafer cookies

In a large bowl, combine cream cheese, butter and extract. Beat with an electric mixer on medium speed until fluffy. Gradually beat in powdered sugar. Stir in chocolate chips. Cover and refrigerate until firm enough to handle, about 2 hours. Roll ball in crushed peppermint candy. Cover and refrigerate for one hour. Serve with graham cracker sticks or wafer cookies. Makes 8 to 10 servings.

Gather up the neighbor kids and go caroling...just for the joy of singing together! Type up lyrics to favorite carols and make enough copies for everyone. Back home, treat everyone to cookies and mugs of hot cocoa.

Together

Denise's Sweet Cream Cheese Spread

Denise Bliss
Milton, NY

This is an office favorite. It's quick & easy to make for a last-minute dip when you're running out the door and you need to bring in something to share for your office friend's birthday! Once you've purchased all the ingredients, any extra dried fruits can be stored in the pantry to make the spread again several more times.

8-oz. container whipped
   cream cheese
1/2 c. caramel ice cream topping
1/2 c. dried cranberries

1/2 c. golden raisins
1/2 c. currants
1/2 c. sliced almonds
sliced pears, apples, crackers

Place container of cream cheese in the center of a serving platter; set aside. In a bowl, mix together caramel topping, dried fruits and nuts; spoon mixture over cream cheese. Arrange sliced fruits and crackers around outside of platter. Serves 8 to 10.

A day or two before your party, set out all the serving platters, baskets and dishes and label them..."chips & dip," "meatballs" and so on. When party time arrives, you'll be able to set out all the goodies in seconds flat.

Very Merry Christmas Trail Mix

Jo Ann Belovitch
Stratford, CT

I like to make this holiday snack mix to give as gifts...it makes a lot! I package it in cellophane Christmas bags tied with colorful ribbons or Christmas treat tins or boxes.

11-1/2 oz. can mixed nuts
11-1/2 oz. can peanuts
11-1/2 oz. can honey-roasted mixed nuts
11-1/2 oz. can honey-roasted peanuts
10-oz. can honey-roasted cashews

12.6-oz. pkg. candy-coated chocolates
3-oz. pkg. chocolate-covered peanuts
3-oz. pkg. chocolate-covered raisins
1-1/2 c. raisins

Combine all ingredients in a very large bowl or roasting pan. Toss to mix; store in airtight containers. Makes about 16 cups.

As Christmas nears, plan a family slumber party! Set up quilts and sleeping bags around the tree, pass around lots of snacks and watch a holiday movie. Before everyone drifts off, read "The Night Before Christmas" by the lights of the Christmas tree. Memories in the making!

Together

Nutty Cranberry Snack Mix

JoAnn
Gooseberry Patch

Mmm...a crunchy snack mix that tastes like cranberry-nut bread.

6 c. bite-size crispy rice cereal
   squares with cinnamon
1 c. walnut halves
1/4 c. frozen orange juice
   concentrate, thawed

1/4 c. brown sugar, packed
2 T. oil
1/2 c. sweetened dried
   cranberries

Combine cereal and walnuts in a large microwave-safe bowl; set aside.
In a microwave-safe bowl, combine orange juice concentrate, brown
sugar and oil. Microwave, uncovered, on high for one minute; stir.
Microwave for one minute longer, stirring after 30 seconds, until hot.
Pour over cereal mixture; stir until evenly coated. Microwave on
high for 5 minutes, stirring every 2 minutes. Stir in cranberries.
Spread on wax paper or aluminum foil to cool. Store in a tightly
covered container. Makes 8 cups.

Package your homemade goodies like crunchy snack mix or
sweet spiced nuts in gift bags tied with ribbon. Set several
in a basket by the door so there will always be a treat
waiting for guests to take home.

Mock Eggnog

Donna Wilson
Maryville, TN

We enjoy this eggnog for the holidays every year, and everyone loves it! It tastes so creamy and delicious, you'd never guess it isn't made with eggs. Top servings with an extra sprinkle of nutmeg.

2 qts. whole or 2% milk
3.4-oz. pkg. instant vanilla
   pudding mix
1/4 c. sugar

1 t. nutmeg
1 t. vanilla extract
1 c. whipping cream

In a large bowl, beat milk and pudding mix with an electric mixer on low speed for 2 minutes. Reduce speed to low. Beat in sugar, nutmeg and vanilla; set aside. In a separate bowl, using clean beaters and electric mixer set on high speed, beat cream until thickened. Add cream to milk mixture; stir together. Cover and refrigerate until serving time. Makes 12 servings.

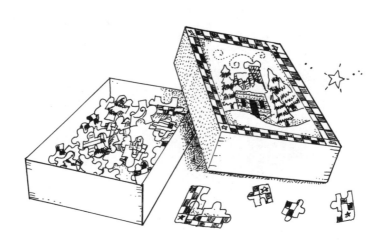

Lay out a Christmas-themed jigsaw puzzle on a table near the fireplace...party guests are sure to enjoy fitting a few pieces into place as they relax with a plateful of appetizers.

Sally's Spiced Cider

Debra Clark
La Mirada, CA

I first tasted this cider this at my sister-in-law Sally's house at Christmastime. I'm very happy she shared the recipe with me.

8 c. apple juice
3 c. cranberry juice cocktail
1 t. whole cloves

1 t. whole allspice
6 4-inch cinnamon sticks
1 orange, quartered

Combine fruit juices in a 4-quart slow cooker. Place cloves and allspice in a tea ball. Add to juice mixture along with cinnamon sticks and orange wedges. Cover and cook on high setting for 30 minutes, or until heated through. Discard spices before serving. Makes 10 to 12 servings.

From autumn through Christmas, a mug of spiced cider will warm you through & through. If you enjoy making it often, save time by filling small muslin bags ahead of time with the whole spices, then just toss into a pot of cider as needed.

Baked Spiced Nuts

Gladys Brehm
Quakertown, PA

A nice touch for a holiday party.

1 egg white
1 t. cold water
1 lb. pecan or walnut halves
1/2 c. sugar

1/2 t. cinnamon
1/2 t. salt
2 to 3 T. butter, melted

In a bowl, beat egg white and water until frothy. Add nuts; stir until well coated. Mix together sugar, cinnamon and salt; sprinkle over nuts and mix well to coat. Coat a 15"x10" jelly-roll pan with melted butter. Spread nuts in pan in a single layer. Bake at 225 degrees for one hour, stirring every 15 minutes. Cool; store in a covered container. Makes about 3 cups.

Spiced nuts are a welcome treat at parties...
perfect for tossing over a winter salad of lettuce,
apples and cranberries too!

FIRESIDE
Soups &
Breads

Chicken Tortilla Soup

Stephanie Howley
Tuckahoe, NY

This slow-cooker recipe is a keeper! I try a new recipe almost every day, so to make something twice is a rare occasion in our home. The corn tortillas thicken the broth to make this a hearty meal.

4 to 6 boneless, skinless
  chicken thighs
2 14-oz. cans chicken broth
1 onion, chopped
1/2 c. salsa
15-oz. can chickpeas

10-oz. pkg. frozen corn
3 6-inch corn tortillas,
  cut into strips
1 t. dried oregano
2 tomatoes, chopped
Optional: chopped fresh cilantro

Combine all ingredients except tomatoes and cilantro in a 5-quart slow cooker; stir. Cover and cook on low setting for 5 to 7 hours, until chicken is tender. Remove chicken and shred with a fork; stir back into soup. Stir in tomatoes just before serving. Garnish with cilantro, if desired. Makes 6 servings.

Top your favorite spicy soup with crunchy tortilla strips.
Brush tortillas with olive oil on both sides. With a pizza cutter,
cut the tortillas into narrow strips. Place strips on a baking
sheet and bake at 375 degrees for 5 to 7 minutes,
turning once or twice, until crisp and golden.

Soups & Breads

Snow-Day Tortellini Soup

Dina Willard
Abingdon, MD

This soup is our daughter's favorite...so very easy and yummy!
Warms you up and makes enough for leftovers the next day. I keep
all the ingredients on hand, so whenever there's a snow day from
school, I'm ready with a hearty lunch for everyone.

2 32-oz. containers chicken
   broth
2 15-oz. jars Alfredo sauce
14-oz. jar roasted red peppers,
   drained and chopped
16-oz. pkg. frozen chopped
   spinach

12-oz. pkg. frozen mini
   meatballs
20-oz. pkg. cheese tortellini,
   uncooked
Garnish: grated Parmesan
   cheese

In a large soup pot, combine all ingredients except tortellini and
garnish. Bring to a boil over high heat; reduce heat to medium. Simmer
for 20 to 30 minutes, until meatballs are cooked through. In a separate
pot, cook tortellini according to package directions. Drain tortellini; add
to soup and heat through. Serve topped with Parmesan cheese. Makes
6 to 8 servings.

Ahhh, soup & bread! Stop by the bakery for a fresh loaf.
Warmed slightly in the oven and topped with real butter,
it's heavenly with any dinner.

Rosemary Turkey Soup

Jaime Gillman
Lawrence, KS

I came up with this soup on a cold day with items I had on hand.
It turned out wonderful...even my husband, who doesn't care
much for soup, loves it! Serve with your favorite dinner rolls.

4 to 5 14-1/2 oz. cans chicken
   broth
6 to 8 carrots, peeled and sliced
2 to 3 stalks celery, sliced,
   including some leafy tops
1/2 t. poultry seasoning

1/2 t. dried thyme
1/2 t. ground sage
1-1/2 t. dried rosemary
1-1/2 lbs. ground turkey
1/2 c. yellow onion, diced
1 to 2 potatoes, peeled

In a large saucepan, combine chicken broth, carrots, celery and
seasonings. Cook over medium-low heat for 10 minutes. Meanwhile,
cook turkey in a stockpot over medium heat until mostly browned;
drain. Pour broth mixture over turkey; add onion. Simmer over low
heat for 30 minutes to one hour. Cover whole potatoes with water in
a separate saucepan, to prevent soup from getting too starchy. Cook
potatoes over high heat until tender; drain. Dice cooled potatoes
and add to soup. Simmer for 10 to 15 minutes more. Makes
10 to 12 servings.

A jar of dried, minced onion can be a real timesaver! If the recipe
has a lot of liquid, such as soups and stews, it's easy to switch.
Just substitute one tablespoon of dried, minced onion for every
1/3 cup diced fresh onion.

Soups & Breads

Beefy Corn & Black Bean Chili

Joyceann Dreibelbis
Wooster, OH

Super quick & easy! Tastes like it's been simmering all day. Use canned beans and frozen corn, if you like...works just as well.

1 lb. ground beef
1 T. chili powder
12-oz. pkg. frozen seasoned
  corn and black beans
14-oz. can low-sodium beef
  broth

15-oz. can chili-seasoned
  tomato sauce
Optional: sour cream, sliced
  green onions, chopped fresh
  cilantro

Combine beef and chili powder in a large Dutch oven. Cook over medium-high heat for 6 minutes, or until beef is browned, stirring to crumble. Drain; stir in frozen corn mixture, beef broth and tomato sauce; bring to a boil. Reduce heat to medium-low. Cover and simmer for 10 minutes. Uncover; simmer 5 more minutes, stirring occasionally. Ladle chili into bowls. Top servings with sour cream, onions and cilantro, as desired. Makes 6 servings.

Cheddar Cheese Bread

Sharman Hess
Asheville, NC

What a delicious bread served with soups and chili! This can be easily doubled for a 13"x9" pan. It's always a hit at bake sales.

1 egg, beaten
1/2 c. milk
1-1/2 c. biscuit baking mix
2 T. dried parsley

1 T. onion, minced
1-1/2 c. shredded Cheddar
  cheese, divided
1/4 c. butter, melted

In a bowl, whisk together egg and milk. Add biscuit mix, parsley, onion and 3/4 cup cheese to make a stiff batter. Spoon batter into a greased 8"x8" baking pan. Sprinkle with remaining cheese; drizzle with melted butter. Bake at 350 degrees for 25 minutes, or until golden. Serves 4 to 6.

Broccoli Cheese & Rice Soup

Lu Madru
Carlisle, AR

I won the grand prize at our local Prairie Rice Cook-Off with this recipe I came up with. It is deeelicious! I live in Prairie County, which is rice country here in Arkansas.

5-1/4 c. boiling water
5 cubes chicken bouillon
1/2 c. butter
1/4 c. onion, chopped
16-oz. pkg frozen chopped
   broccoli
1 lb. pasteurized process cheese
   spread, cubed

2 c. milk
1 t. garlic powder
3 c. cooked long-grain white rice
2 4-oz. cans mushroom stems &
   pieces, drained and chopped
2/3 c. cornstarch
1 c. cold water

Combine boiling water and bouillon cubes; let stand until dissolved. Meanwhile, in a large saucepan, melt butter over medium heat. Cook onion in butter until softened. Stir in broccoli; add hot chicken broth. Simmer until broccoli is tender, 10 to 15 minutes. Reduce heat to low; stir in cheese cubes until melted. Stir in milk, garlic powder, cooked rice and mushrooms. In a small bowl, stir cornstarch into cold water until dissolved. Stir cornstarch mixture into soup. Cook, stirring often, until thickened. Makes 12 servings.

A "souper" gift for a new bride! Fill a roomy stockpot with all the fixin's for a warming soup supper...a ladle, soup seasonings and a big jar of your best warm-you-to-your-toes soup! Be sure to include a copy of the recipe too.

Soups & Breads

Best-Ever Potato Soup

Sue Neely
Greenville, IL

This is a great soup to warm you up on a chilly night. You'll love the rich, cheesy taste. Serve with oyster crackers or your favorite bread.

8 slices bacon, diced
14-1/2 oz. can chicken broth
3 c. potatoes, peeled and cubed
1 carrot, peeled and grated or
    finely chopped
1 to 2 stalks celery, chopped
1/2 onion, chopped
1 T. dried parsley

1/2 t. salt
1/2 t. pepper
3 c. milk
1/4 c. all-purpose flour
8-oz. pkg. American cheese,
    cubed
Optional: 3 green onions, thinly
    chopped

Cook bacon in a large skillet over medium heat; drain. Transfer bacon to a large soup pot; add chicken broth, vegetables and seasonings. Cover and simmer over medium heat until potatoes are tender, about 15 minutes. In a small bowl, stir together milk and flour until smooth; add to soup. Bring to a boil; boil and stir for 2 minutes. Add cheese; cook and stir until cheese is melted and soup is heated through. Garnish with green onions, if desired. Makes 8 servings.

A snowy winter afternoon is the perfect time to daydream about next year's flower and vegetable gardens. With a savory soup simmering on the stove, you'll have some free time to start leafing through seed and plant catalogs.

Christmas Eve Ham Soup

Susan Govig
Madrid, IA

We make this recipe every Christmas Eve to eat before we go to the service at church. It's always a great family time when we can share fond memories of the past year.

2 c. potatoes, peeled and diced
1/2 c. carrots, peeled and diced
1/2 c. celery, diced
1/4 c. onion, chopped
3 c. water
1-1/2 t. salt
1/4 t. pepper

1 c. cooked ham, cubed
1/4 c. butter
1/4 c. all-purpose flour
2 c. milk
8-oz. pkg. shredded Cheddar
  cheese

Combine vegetables, water, salt and pepper in a large soup pot. Bring to a boil over medium heat. Reduce heat to medium-low; cover and simmer until vegetables are tender. Stir in ham; set aside. In a separate saucepan, melt butter over low heat; stir in flour until smooth. Gradually add milk; bring to a boil. Cook and stir for 2 minutes, or until thickened. Stir in cheese until melted; add to vegetable mixture and heat through. This soup also reheats very well. Makes 8 servings.

Hosting a holiday meal for family & friends? Hang a homespun stocking filled with goodies on the back of each chair for instant country charm!

Soups & Breads

Chicken & Barley Soup

Geneva Rogers
Gillette, WY

*I love chicken soup in the winter, and barley makes
a nice change from noodles or rice.*

4 chicken thighs
1-1/2 t. salt, divided
3/4 t. pepper, divided
1 T. olive oil
2 carrots, peeled and sliced
2 stalks celery, sliced

1 onion, chopped
10 c. chicken broth
1/2 c. pearl barley, uncooked
1/2 c. fresh parsley, chopped
1 t. lemon zest
Garnish: lemon wedges

Season chicken with 1/2 teaspoon salt and 1/4 teaspoon pepper;
set aside. Heat oil in a large soup pot over medium-high heat. Add
chicken, skin-side down. Cook for 7 to 8 minutes, until skin is golden
but chicken isn't cooked through. Transfer chicken to a plate, reserving
drippings in pot. Add vegetables to reserved drippings; season with
1/2 teaspoon salt and 1/4 teaspoon pepper. Cook until tender, stirring
occasionally. Add chicken broth and barley; return chicken to pot.
Bring to a boil; reduce heat to medium-low. Cover and simmer until
barley is tender and chicken is cooked through, 30 to 40 minutes.
Meanwhile, combine parsley, lemon zest and remaining salt and pepper
in a small bowl. Transfer chicken to a plate and shred, discarding skin
and bones. Return chicken to soup pot. Serve bowls of soup topped
with a spoonful of parsley mixture and lemon wedges on the side.
Makes 6 servings.

For a festive garnish on bowls of hot soup, use a mini
cookie cutter to cut star shapes from slices of cheese.

Hamburger Soup

Janae Mallonee
Marlboro, MA

This has been a go-to easy soup in my family for generations. The recipe isn't exact, but those recipes never are! Tweak the seasonings until it is right for your palate. I serve mine with a sprinkle of Parmesan cheese on the top...mmm. Hubby and darling daughter like theirs with a dash of hot sauce.

1 lb. ground beef
6 c. beef broth
10-oz. pkg. frozen mixed
  vegetables
1 c. onion, diced
Italian seasoning and pepper
  to taste

1 c. pastina or other small soup
  pasta, uncooked
Optional: grated Parmesan
  cheese, hot pepper sauce

Brown beef in a soup pot over medium heat; drain. Add broth and bring to a boil; add frozen vegetables, onion and seasonings. Stir in uncooked pasta. Simmer for 20 minutes, stirring occasionally. Garnish as desired. Makes 4 to 6 servings.

Savory Bread Sticks

Amy Mauseth
Reno, NV

A flavorful change of pace for biscuit lovers.

1/2 c. grated Parmesan cheese
2 t. garlic, minced
1/4 t. red pepper flakes

7-1/2 oz. tube refrigerated
  biscuits
2 T. olive oil

In a shallow bowl, combine cheese, garlic and pepper; set aside. Roll each biscuit into a 6-inch rope. Brush each rope with olive oil; roll in cheese mixture to coat. Twist ropes a few times and place onto a greased baking sheet. Bake at 400 degrees for 8 to 10 minutes, until golden. Makes 8 bread sticks.

Tiny pasta shapes like orzo and stars are quick-cooking and ideal
for making soup. Or substitute alphabets, just for fun.

Soups & Breads

Oh-So-Easy Beef Stew

Diana Chaney
Olathe, KS

I love being able to put together this slow-cooker stew in the morning, then continue on my busy day of decorating, shopping and other holiday activities. At dinnertime, the stew is all ready for my hungry family! Serve with warm biscuits or crusty bread.

2 16-oz. pkgs. frozen stew
    vegetables
1-1/2 lbs. stew beef cubes
10-3/4 oz. tomato soup

10-3/4 oz. can cream of
    mushroom or celery soup
1.35-oz. pkg. onion soup mix

Add frozen vegetables to a 6-quart slow cooker. Top with beef cubes; set aside. In a bowl, stir together soups and soup mix; spoon over beef. Cover and cook on low setting for 7 to 8 hours. Makes 6 servings.

Invite friends over for a soup supper on a frosty winter evening.
Ask everyone to bring their favorite soup or bread to share...
you provide the bowls, spoons and a crackling fire!

Kielbasa Bean Soup

Nicole Dixon
Fort Madison, IA

This recipe is so easy and delicious! Serve with hot dinner rolls.

1/2 white onion, chopped
2/3 c. celery, chopped
1 T. butter
5 c. water, divided
2 16-oz. cans whole potatoes,
    drained and diced

14-1/2 oz. can sliced carrots,
    drained
12-oz. pkg. Kielbasa sausage,
    diced
2 10-3/4 oz. cans bean &
    bacon soup

In a large saucepan over medium heat, sauté onion and celery in butter for 10 minutes. Add 3 cups water. Bring to a boil; reduce heat to medium-low and simmer for 45 minutes. Stir in remaining water and other ingredients. Cook over low heat, stirring occasionally, for 30 minutes. Makes 4 to 6 servings.

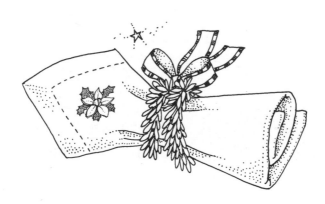

Make mini wreaths of pine-scented rosemary to slip around dinner napkins. Simply wind fresh rosemary stems into a ring shape, tuck in the ends and tie on a tiny bow...so festive!

Soups & Breads

White Bean Soup

Paige Bear
Lyman, SC

*My girls love this soup on a cold day. I serve it with grilled ham
sandwiches. It's equally good topped with herbed croutons.*

1/3 c. white onion, chopped
2 T. olive oil
1 clove garlic, minced
3 T. all-purpose flour or
    rice flour
2 14-1/2 oz. cans chicken broth

2 16-oz. cans white beans,
    drained and rinsed
4-inch sprig fresh rosemary
1/4 t. kosher salt
1/4 t. pepper

In a soup pot, sauté onion in olive oil over medium-high heat. Add
garlic; cook and stir for 30 seconds. Sprinkle with flour; cook and stir
until flour is blended with onion mixture. Whisk in chicken broth;
add beans and rosemary. Bring to a boil over medium heat; reduce
heat to medium-low. Simmer for 30 minutes, stirring occasionally.
At serving time, discard rosemary sprig; season with salt and pepper.
Makes 6 servings.

Add an extra can or two of soup, vegetables or tuna to the grocery
cart every week, then put aside these extras at home. Before you
know it, you'll have a generous selection of canned goods for
the local food pantry. A terrific lesson for kids to share in!

Christmas Chicken & Rice Soup
Judy Phelan
Macomb, IL

Christmas Eve day has always been a busy day in our household. This warm and comforting slow-cooker soup is a yearly tradition and simplifies the busy holiday meal for us.

4-1/2 c. chicken broth
2 c. water
1 c. carrots, peeled and grated
1 c. celery, diced
2 boneless, skinless chicken
   breasts
6.2-oz. pkg. quick-cooking long
   grain and wild rice mix

1/2 c. all-purpose flour
1/2 t. salt
1/2 t. pepper
1/2 c. butter, sliced
2 c. half-and-half

In a large slow cooker, combine chicken broth, water, carrots, celery, chicken and rice mix with seasoning packet. Cover and cook on low setting for 6 to 8 hours, or on high setting for 4 to 6 hours. Remove chicken to a plate; shred with 2 forks and return to slow cooker. In a small bowl, combine flour, salt and pepper; set aside. Melt butter in a saucepan over medium heat. Gradually stir flour mixture into melted butter; cook and stir until golden. Gradually stir in half-and-half until smooth and well blended. Stir half-and-half mixture into soup in slow cooker; cover and cook for 15 more minutes. Makes 6 servings.

Be sure to ask your children about their favorite foods for the Christmas season. You may find you have "traditions" in your own family that you weren't even aware of.

Soups & Breads

Homestyle Chicken Noodle Soup

Sharon Murray
Lexington Park, MD

Delicious and so easy! For a shortcut, use a deli rotisserie chicken.

3 boneless, skinless chicken
  breasts
10 to 12 c. water
6 cubes chicken bouillon
2 10-3/4 oz. cans cream of
  chicken soup

1/2 c. dried, chopped onion
5 to 6 carrots, peeled and
  chopped
2 to 3 stalks celery, chopped
16-oz. pkg. egg noodles,
  uncooked

Place chicken in a saucepan; add enough water to cover. Cook over medium heat until tender, 15 to 20 minutes. Drain; cube chicken and set aside. Meanwhile, in a soup pot, combine 10 to 12 cups water and bouillon cubes; bring to a boil over high heat. Whisk in canned soup and onion; return to a boil. Reduce heat to medium. Add carrots and celery; cook until tender. Add noodles; cook until noodles are nearly tender. Stir in cubed chicken; cook until noodles are tender. Makes 4 to 6 servings.

Cindy's Nut Bread

Cindy Lyzenga
Zeeland, MI

This is my go-to recipe for quick bread, as the ingredients are always on hand. I often make two small loaves for gift giving.

3 c. all-purpose flour
1 c. sugar
4 t. baking powder
1 t. salt

1 egg, beaten
1-2/3 c. milk
1/4 c. oil
3/4 c. chopped nuts

In a large bowl, stir together flour, sugar, baking powder and salt; set aside. In a separate bowl, whisk together egg, milk and oil. Add to flour mixture, stirring just until combined. Stir in nuts. Turn batter into a greased 9"x5" loaf pan. Bake at 350 degrees for one hour to one hour and 15 minutes. Cool in pan for 10 minutes. Turn out of pan; cool on a rack. Wrap and store overnight before slicing. Freezes well. Makes one loaf.

Pat's Very Good Soup

Pat Minnich
El Cajon, CA

*This is a great slow-cooker recipe made with leftover turkey
or ham from the Christmas feast. A tasty and different way
to use your leftovers!*

3/4 c. onion, chopped
2 t. oil
1 lb. cooked turkey or ham,
   chopped
4 c. cocktail vegetable juice
15-oz. can ranch-style beans
14-1/2 oz. can stewed tomatoes
10-oz. can diced tomatoes with
   green chiles

16-oz. can pinto beans, drained
15-1/2 oz. can white hominy,
   drained
15-oz. can corn, drained
1-oz. pkg. ranch salad dressing
   mix
Garnish: shredded Cheddar
   cheese, sour cream,
   tortilla chips

In a skillet, sauté onion in oil. Drain and transfer to a 6-quart slow
cooker. Add remaining ingredients except garnish; stir well. Cover and
cook on low setting for 6 to 8 hours. Serve in soup bowls, garnished
as desired. Makes 8 servings.

Slow-cooker meals are perfect after a day of Christmas shopping
or decorating. For an easy side, whip up a marinated salad to
keep in the fridge...cut up crunchy veggies and toss with
zesty Italian salad dressing.

Soups & Breads

White Bean & Sausage Soup

Jo Ann
Gooseberry Patch

We like to keep the New Year's Day tradition of beans and pork for luck. But after all the elaborate holiday meals and goodies, I wanted something much simpler. This fits the bill! It's tossed together in the morning, then simmers all day while we watch the parades and bowl games on television. Serve with crusty bread and butter.

6 c. water
1.8-oz. pkg. leek soup mix
1 lb. Kielbasa sausage, sliced
2 15-oz. cans cannellini beans,
   drained

6-oz. pkg. fresh Swiss chard
   or spinach, torn
Garnish: shredded Parmesan
   cheese

Combine water and soup mix in a 4-quart slow cooker. Add sausage and beans. Cover and cook on low setting for 7 to 9 hours. Stir in Swiss chard or spinach into soup in slow cooker. Cover and cook for 10 minutes, or just until wilted. Serve topped with Parmesan cheese. Serves 5 to 6.

A quick & easy way to thicken bean soup...purée a cup of the soup in a blender or even mash it in a bowl, then stir it back into the soup pot.

New England Clam Chowder

Michele Coen
Delevan, NY

*My family loves this chowder...it's always a big hit
at our family gatherings.*

2 to 3 6-1/2 oz. cans minced
   clams, drained and liquid
   reserved
2 c. potatoes, peeled and diced
1 c. celery, chopped
1/2 c. onion, chopped

3/4 t. salt
1/8 t. pepper
3 c. milk
1/4 c. all-purpose flour
Garnish: saltine crackers

In a large saucepan, combine reserved clam liquid, vegetables, salt and pepper. Bring to a boil over medium heat; reduce heat to low. Cover and simmer for 10 minutes. Pour milk into a jar with a tight-fitting lid; add flour and shake until blended. Gradually stir milk into vegetable mixture. Cook over medium heat, stirring often, for 15 minutes. Stir in clams; heat through over low heat, stirring often. Do not boil. Serve with crackers. Makes 4 to 6 servings.

Tomato Shrimp Soup

Janet Elwick
Vinton, IA

*Our family enjoys this simple yet elegant soup. It's the
perfect thing to warm you from the inside-out, especially on
a cold winter night here in Iowa.*

10-3/4 oz. can tomato soup
1-1/4 c. 2% milk
1 t. sugar

1 t. curry powder
4-oz. can small shrimp,
   drained and rinsed

Combine all ingredients in a saucepan over medium heat.
Cook, stirring occasionally, until heated through.
Makes 4 servings.

A swirl of cream is a tasty garnish for a
bowl of creamy soup. Add a sprinkle of
chopped fresh parsley.

CREAM

Soups & Breads

Quick Fish Chowder

Mary Lou Thomas
Portland, ME

For real New England chowder, cut the fish into large pieces. It will become flaky as it cooks. Garnish with a sprinkle of paprika.

2 T. butter
2 c. frozen onion, celery and
   carrot mix
2 c. potatoes, peeled and diced
2 c. clam juice or chicken broth

1 t. salt
1/2 t. pepper
1 lb. haddock fillet, cut into
   chunks
1 c. whole milk

Melt butter in a large saucepan over medium heat. Add frozen vegetables; cook until onion is translucent. Add potatoes, juice or broth, salt and pepper. Cover and simmer for 10 to 15 minutes, until vegetables are tender. Reduce heat to medium-low. Add fish; cook for 10 minutes longer. Stir in milk; heat through but do not boil. Makes 4 servings.

Savory herbed crackers make any bowl of soup even yummier! Toss together 1-1/2 cups oyster crackers, 1-1/2 tablespoons melted butter, 1/4 teaspoon dried thyme and 1/4 teaspoon garlic powder. Spread on a baking sheet. Bake at 350 degrees for about 10 minutes, until crunchy and golden.

Elizabeth's Prize-Winning Chili

Vickie Wiseman
Hamilton, OH

Elizabeth is my 13-year-old granddaughter. This recipe has won her a first-place prize in two different chili cook-offs. She started cooking when she was five years old and now she's my assistant in the children's cooking class I teach at our church.

1 lb. ground beef
1 lb. ground pork sausage
3/4 c. onion, diced
1 T. garlic, minced
1/2 green pepper, chopped
1/2 red pepper, chopped
1/2 orange pepper, chopped
1/2 yellow pepper, chopped
2 28-oz. cans diced tomatoes
1/2 c. chili powder
1/4 c. ground cumin

1 t. dried oregano
1 t. dried parsley
1 t. dried thyme
1 t. dried sage
1 t. cinnamon
2 15-oz. cans kidney beans, drained and rinsed
8-oz. can tomato sauce
Optional: shredded Cheddar cheese

Brown beef and sausage in a large skillet over medium heat; drain. Add onion, garlic and peppers; cook until onion is translucent. Add tomatoes with juice; bring to a boil. Stir in spices, beans and tomato sauce. Reduce heat to low. Simmer for 45 minutes, stirring occasionally. Serve bowls of chili topped with cheese, if desired. Makes 10 to 12 servings.

December is jam-packed with shopping, decorating, baking... take it easy with simple, hearty meals. Make double batches of family favorites like chili or Sloppy Joes early in the holiday season and freeze half to heat and eat later. You'll be so glad you did!

Hearty Vegetable-Beef Soup

Nancy Gasko
South Bend, IN

I have made this soup for more than 35 years. It's been changed and improved on, until it's now this terrific recipe that everyone likes. Since it simmers for hours, it's perfect for a day when you're trimming the tree, wrapping gifts or simply enjoying a snow day indoors. Serve with fresh bread and a crisp salad.

3 lbs. stew beef cubes
2 to 3 T. oil
2 46-oz. containers beef broth
46-oz. bottle cocktail vegetable
  juice
28-oz. can crushed tomatoes
2 to 3 c. water
2 16-oz. pkgs. frozen mixed
  soup vegetables
4 c. potatoes, peeled and diced
2 c. onion, diced

1-1/2 c. celery, diced
1-1/2 c. carrots, peeled
  and diced
1/2 c. long-cooking barley,
  uncooked
1 to 2 T. beef soup base
1 T. garlic, minced
1 T. Worcestershire sauce
1/2 t. chili powder
6 whole allspice
4 bay leaves

In a large soup pot over medium heat, brown beef in oil; drain. Stir in remaining ingredients, enclosing allspice and bay leaves in a spice bag, if desired. Bring to a boil; reduce heat to low. Cover and simmer for 4 to 6 hours, stirring occasionally. Discard allspice and bay leaves before serving. Makes 10 to 12 servings.

When vacationing throughout the year, look for Christmas ornaments for the tree. Come December, they're sure to bring great memories of family travels and fun!

Amazing Vegetable Tortellini Soup

Judith Jennings
Ironwood, MI

Wonderful to eat on a chilly day! I like to add some Italian seasoning and rosemary-garlic seasoning to taste. These additions really give it some zip!

4 carrots, peeled and chopped
1 c. onion, chopped
1 T. olive oil
4 cloves garlic, minced
4 14-1/2 oz. cans low-sodium
   vegetable broth
14-1/2 oz. can diced tomatoes
   with garlic, basil & oregano

3 small zucchini, chopped
1/2 c. fresh spinach, chopped
1/3 c. medium salsa
1/4 t. dried rosemary
1/4 t. pepper
24-oz. pkg. cheese tortellini,
   uncooked
1 T. red wine vinegar

In a Dutch oven over medium heat, sauté carrots and onion in olive oil until onion is tender. Add garlic; cook one minute longer. Stir in vegetable broth, tomatoes with juice, zucchini, spinach, salsa and seasonings. Bring to a boil; add tortellini. Reduce heat to medium-low. Cover and simmer for 8 to 10 minutes, until tortellini are tender. Stir in vinegar just before serving. Serves 10 to 12.

Take a Christmas photo of your family in the same place, same position each year, for example in the front of the tree...a sweet record of how the kids have grown!

Soups & Breads

Potato & Corn Chowder

Dee Gilbert
Blackstone, MA

I made this chowder for the first time over 15 years ago, and it was an immediate hit. My kids still ask for it when the cold winter days come! Serve alone or with sandwiches for a delicious, filling meal.

6 to 8 baking potatoes, peeled
4 14-3/4 oz. cans creamed corn
2 14-1/2 oz. cans corn
4 c. fat-free half-and-half

2 c. 2% milk
1/8 t. cayenne pepper
pepper to taste

Cover whole potatoes with water in a large stockpot. Cook over high heat until just soft; drain. Cut potatoes into bite-size cubes; return to stockpot. Add remaining ingredients; bring just to a boil over medium-high heat. Reduce heat to low. Cook, stirring often, for 10 minutes. Makes 10 servings.

2-4-1 Drop Biscuits

Crystal Shook
Catawba, NC

These are so simple! Serve warm with butter and jam.

2 c. self-rising flour
1/4 c. shortening

1 c. milk

Combine all ingredients in a large bowl; mix well. Drop dough by tablespoonfuls onto a greased baking sheet. Bake at 350 degrees for 20 to 25 minutes, until golden. Makes one dozen.

Keep fresh-baked bread warm and toasty...simply slip a piece of aluminum foil into a bread basket, then top it with a decorative napkin.

Italian Pasta & Bean Soup

Diane Cohen
Breinigsville, PA

Very quick & easy! Delicious with cornbread or grilled cheese.

1 T. olive oil
3/4 c. onion, chopped
2 T. garlic, minced
6 c. reduced-sodium chicken
  broth
1 T. Italian seasoning

1-1/2 c. farfalline pasta or elbow
  macaroni, uncooked
14-1/2 oz. can diced tomatoes
2 15-oz. cans cannellini beans,
  drained and rinsed
1/4 c. grated Parmesan cheese

Heat olive oil in a soup pot over medium-high heat. Add onion; sauté
for 5 minutes, or until soft and golden. Add garlic; cook and stir for
one minute. Add chicken broth and seasoning; bring to a boil. Add
pasta and cook for 5 minutes. Stir in tomatoes with juice and beans;
cook for 4 more minutes, or until pasta is tender. Stir in cheese just
before serving. Serves 6 to 8.

Blue Cheese Muffins

Mia Rossi
Charlotte, NC

These savory mini muffins will jazz up any bowl of soup.

2 c. self-rising flour
1/2 c. butter
1/2 c. crumbled blue cheese

1 t. ground sage
8-oz. container sour cream
1/4 c. milk

Add flour and butter to a large bowl. Cut butter into flour with a pastry
blender or 2 forks until crumbly. Add remaining ingredients; stir just
until moistened. Spoon batter into 24 greased mini muffin cups. Bake
at 400 degrees for 15 to 18 minutes, until lightly golden. Serve warm.
Makes 2 dozen.

Soups & Breads

Creamy Tomato Soup

April Constantine
Story, WY

On snowy evenings, my family loves this quick & easy soup, accompanied by gooey grilled cheese sandwiches. If you like your tomato soup chunky, use just one can of puréed tomatoes and add a can of petite diced tomatoes.

3/4 c. onion, diced
2 T. butter
2 28-oz. cans Italian-style
　　tomato purée
2 10-3/4 oz. cans tomato soup
1-1/2 c. milk

1 t. sugar
1/2 t. paprika
Optional: 1/2 c. cooking sherry
8-oz. pkg cream cheese,
　　softened and cubed

In a soup pot over medium heat, sauté onion in butter until softened. Stir in tomatoes with juice, soup, milk, sugar, paprika and sherry, if using. Bring to a boil. Reduce heat to low; cover and simmer for 10 minutes. Stir in cream cheese until melted. Makes 10 to 12 servings.

Throw an impromptu sledding party for the first snowfall! Gather friends & neighbors to enjoy some snow fun and then head back home for a cozy fire and mugs of hot cocoa or mulled cider.

Warm Winter Soup

M'lissa Johnson
Baytown, TX

My whole family loves to eat this soup in front of the fireplace! It's a great soup for cold winter days. It's a combination of several different recipes that I've played with over the years. This soup freezes well.

1 lb. stew beef cubes
1 T. oil
6 slices bacon, chopped
1/4 c. onion, chopped
1 c. celery, chopped
2 cloves garlic, minced
14-1/2 oz. can Italian stewed
    tomatoes
4 c. spicy vegetable cocktail juice

14-1/2 oz. can beef broth
4 carrots, peeled and chopped
1 zucchini, peeled and chopped
1-1/2 c. water
2 t. fresh basil, chopped
1 bay leaf
1 t. salt
24-oz. pkg. cheese tortellini,
    uncooked

In a skillet over medium heat, brown beef in oil. Remove beef to a plate; add bacon, onion, celery and garlic to skillet. Cook until bacon is crisp and vegetables are tender. Transfer contents of skillet to a 5-quart slow cooker; add beef. Stir in tomatoes with juice and remaining ingredients except tortellini. Cover and cook on low setting for 6 to 8 hours. About 20 minutes before serving, add tortellini; continue cooking until tortellini are tender. Discard bay leaf before serving. Makes 8 servings.

Watch tag sales for a big red speckled enamelware stockpot...
it's just the right size for cooking up a family-size batch of soup.
The bright color adds a homey touch to any soup supper!

Garden Harvest Chicken Stew

Tina Butler
Royse City, TX

Chicken stew is popular in the south, and this slow-cooker version is great for cold days. Just use whatever vegetables you have on hand.

2 T. olive oil
3 to 4 boneless, skinless chicken
    breasts, cubed
salt and pepper to taste
3 c. low-sodium chicken broth,
    divided
6 potatoes, peeled and cubed
4 to 5 carrots, peeled and
    sliced thin

1 c. fresh or frozen green beans,
    trimmed
1/2 onion, chopped
1 cube chicken bouillon
1-1/4 c. cold water, divided
6-oz. can tomato paste
1 bay leaf
1 zucchini, chopped
3 T. cornstarch

Heat olive oil in a large skillet over medium-high heat. Add chicken; season with salt and pepper. Sauté until lightly golden. Transfer chicken to a plate, reserving drippings in skillet. Add 1/2 cup chicken broth to drippings; cook and stir over high heat until hot, scraping up brown bits in skillet. Return chicken to skillet; add vegetables and sauté for 3 to 5 minutes. Transfer mixture to a 6-quart slow cooker; add remaining broth, bouillon cube, one cup water, tomato paste and bay leaf. Cover and cook on low setting for 6 to 7 hours, or on high setting for 4 hours. During the final 2 hours, add zucchini. About 30 minutes before serving, combine remaining water and cornstarch in a cup; stir until smooth. Stir mixture into stew. Cover and cook for an additional 20 minutes, or until thickened. Discard bay leaf before serving. Serves 8.

The most splendid gift, the most marveled and magic,
is the gift that has not yet been opened. Opaque behind
wrapping or winking foil, it is a box full of possibilities.

–Gregg Easterbrook

Fran's Chicken & Rice Soup

Sherri Rollins
Carlisle, AR

When my wonderful friend Frances heard I was ill, she sent me a container of this soup. So sweet of her...and it did the trick!

8 c. chicken broth
1 c. celery, chopped
2 carrots, peeled and chopped
2/3 c. long-cooking rice, uncooked

4 c. cooked chicken breast, diced
14-oz. can cream of mushroom soup
1/2 c. pasteurized process cheese spread, cubed

In a large soup pot over high heat, combine chicken broth, celery and carrots. Bring to a boil; reduce heat to medium and cook until vegetables are tender. Add rice; cover and simmer for 20 minutes. Stir in chicken, canned soup and cheese. Cook and stir until well blended and cheese is melted. Makes 8 to 10 servings.

Homemade chicken soup can't be beat for shaking off a winter cold. For another warming remedy, brew up a pot of ginger tea. Chop a fresh ginger root into 1/2-inch chunks and cover with cold water in a saucepan. Bring to a boil, simmer for 15 to 20 minutes and strain. Sip hot with honey or lemon, if desired. Sure to make you feel better!

Soups & Breads

Speedy Mexican Chicken Soup
*Michelle West
Garland, TX*

I created this recipe out of my love for King Ranch-style chicken casseroles. I love soup and wanted the same great flavor as the casserole, but a little quicker to make.

12-oz. can chicken, flaked
10-3/4 oz. can of cream of
   mushroom soup
10-3/4 oz. cream of chicken
   soup
10-3/4 oz. can diced tomatoes
   with green chiles

14-1/2 oz. can chicken broth
Garnish: shredded Cheddar
   cheese, diced avocado,
   tortilla or corn chips

Add chicken, soups and tomatoes with juice to a soup pot over medium heat. Stir well; add enough chicken broth for desired consistency. Bring to a boil; reduce heat to low. Simmer for about 10 minutes. Ladle into bowls; garnish as desired. Makes 4 servings.

Fiesta Cornbread
*Beckie Apple
Grannis, AR*

There's nothing my family likes better than a warm pan of cornbread fresh from the oven, slathered with creamy butter! Add a bowl of homemade soup or chili, and you have a wonderful meal.

1 c. self-rising yellow
   cornmeal mix
1/4 c. self-rising flour
1/2 t. baking powder
2 T. sugar
1 c. canned creamed corn

1/4 c. oil
2 T. milk
2 eggs, well beaten
2 jalapeño peppers, diced
1 c. shredded Cheddar cheese

Combine cornmeal, flour, baking powder and sugar in a large bowl; stir well to blend. Add remaining ingredients and mix well. Pour batter into a well-greased 8"x8" baking pan. Bake at 400 degrees for 25 minutes, or until golden. Makes 6 to 9 servings.

Chicken Parmesan Soup

Ginny Watson
Scranton, PA

*The flavor of chicken Parmesan in a bowl of hot soup with
a cheesy toast slice. Worth shredding fresh Parmesan cheese for!*

2 boneless, skinless chicken
   breasts
salt and pepper to taste
4 T. olive oil, divided
1 onion, thinly sliced

3 cloves garlic, chopped
28-oz. can diced tomatoes
4 c. chicken broth
1 c. fresh basil, chopped

Place chicken between 2 pieces of plastic wrap; pound to flatten. Cut
chicken into cubes; season with salt and pepper. In a soup pot over
medium heat, sauté chicken in 2 tablespoons olive oil, until just
cooked through. Remove chicken to a plate. Heat remaining oil in
soup pot; add onion and garlic. Cook until onion is softened. Add
tomatoes with juice and chicken broth; bring to a simmer and cook for
about 5 minutes. Return chicken to soup pot; cook for 2 to 3 minutes.
Stir in basil. Meanwhile, make Crisp Toasts. To serve, place one slice
of toast in each bowl; ladle soup over toast. Top with another slice of
toast. Serves 4.

Crisp Toasts:

8 slices crusty bread
2 T. olive oil
salt and pepper to taste

1 clove garlic, halved
1/2 c. shredded Parmesan
   cheese

Drizzle bread with olive oil; season with salt and pepper. Arrange on a
baking sheet. Watching closely, toast bread under a hot broiler until
lightly golden on both sides. Remove from oven; rub each
bread slice with cut sides of garlic. Top with cheese.
Return to broiler for one to 2 minutes,
until cheese is melted.

Fond memories and a glowing fire are
kindred friends...both delight the heart
and warm the home.

–Anonymous

Soups & Breads

Creamy Onion Soup

Denise Webb
Newington, GA

A velvety, delicious soup that's full of comfort. Pair with some crusty bread, and you have a wonderful warm-you-up meal, especially when the weather turns cold.

2 c. sweet onions, thinly sliced
6 T. butter, divided
14-1/2 oz. can chicken broth
2 cubes chicken bouillon
1/4 t. pepper
3 T. all-purpose flour

1-1/2 c. milk
1/4 c. pasteurized process
  cheese, cubed
Garnish: shredded Cheddar
  cheese, minced fresh parsley

In a large skillet over medium-low heat, cook onions in 3 tablespoons butter until tender. Add chicken broth, bouillon cubes and pepper; bring to a boil. Remove from heat; set aside. In a large saucepan over medium heat, melt remaining butter. Stir in flour until smooth; gradually stir in milk. Bring to a boil; cook and stir for one to 2 minutes, until thickened. Reduce heat to low; stir in onion mixture and cubed cheese. Cook and stir until heated through and cheese is melted. Garnish with Cheddar cheese and parsley. Makes 6 to 8 servings.

Soup is extra hearty served in a bread bowl. Cut the tops off round crusty loaves and scoop out the soft bread inside. Brush with olive oil and bake at 350 degrees for a few minutes, until toasty. Ladle in soup...yum!

Winter Vegetable Soup for Two

Christy Huggins
Melbourne, FL

Very simple to make...just enough to share with a friend! It takes the chill off and makes you feel warm and cozy.

1/2 c. green onions, sliced
1 T. oil
14-1/2 oz. can chicken broth
1/4 t. dried thyme
1 large potato, peeled and cubed

1 small carrot, peeled and sliced
1 c. broccoli, chopped
1/4 t. salt
1/8 t. pepper

In a saucepan over medium heat, sauté onions in oil until tender. Add chicken broth, thyme, potato and carrot; bring to a boil. Reduce heat to low. Simmer, uncovered, for about 5 minutes. Add broccoli, salt and pepper. Simmer, uncovered, for about 7 minutes, until vegetables are tender. Serves 2.

Trim Vegetable Soup

Patty Flak
Erie, PA

One of the tastiest "diet" soups I've ever had! Just right for those New Year resolutions.

4 c. water
2 c. tomato juice
3 c. cabbage, finely chopped
3 stalks celery, diced

2 T. dried, chopped onion
1 cube beef bouillon
1/8 t. pepper

Combine all ingredients in a saucepan. Simmer over low heat for one hour. Transfer several spoonfuls of vegetables to a blender. Process until puréed; return to soup. Heat through. Makes 6 servings.

Multi-grain crackers and crunchy bread sticks can round out suppers for one or two. They're perfect paired with soup and salads, and they'll stay fresh much longer than a loaf of bread.

SEASONAL
Salads & Sides

Mixed Greens & Cranberry Salad

Cortney Schrecengost
Blairsville, PA

This salad is wonderful paired with a holiday meal.

4 c. mixed salad greens
1 Granny Smith apple, cored
   and cubed
1/4 c. crumbled blue cheese

1/4 c. sweetened dried
   cranberries
1/4 c. toasted chopped
   pecans

Make Vinaigrette Dressing; set aside. Mix all of the ingredients together in a large salad bowl. Drizzle dressing over salad; toss to mix. Serves 4 to 6.

Vinaigrette Dressing:

1/2 t. Dijon mustard
3 T. champagne vinegar

1 t. sugar
1/2 c. light olive oil

Whisk mustard, vinegar and sugar together while slowly adding the olive oil until mixture is well blended.

Create a charming centerpiece in a jiffy. Arrange several pretty teacups on a cake stand, handles turned into the center. Place a plump candle in each teacup, surround with sprigs of faux evergreen and tuck in a few shiny ornament balls.

Cranberry Mousse

Susan Kruspe
Hall, NY

This is a great accompaniment to a holiday dinner, especially with roast turkey or chicken. The salad adds color and wonderful flavor to any meal. I am asked for the recipe whenever I serve this.

6-oz. pkg. raspberry gelatin mix
1 c. boiling water
20-oz. can crushed pineapple,
   drained and juice reserved

14-oz. can whole-berry
   cranberry sauce
3 T. lemon juice
16-oz. container sour cream

In a large bowl, dissolve gelatin mix in boiling water; add reserved pineapple juice. Stir in cranberry sauce and lemon juice until well mixed. Cover and refrigerate until mixture thickens. Fold in sour cream and pineapple; transfer to an oiled 9-cup mold or a glass serving bowl. Chill until set, at least 2 hours. Makes 16 servings.

Make gift shopping twice as easy year 'round...when you find a useful kitchen utensil or handy household item for yourself, just buy two! Tuck away the extras in a big box for future gift-giving.

Green Bean & Bacon Salad

Jewel Sharpe
Raleigh, NC

Refreshing and easy! The red and green colors look
so festive at Christmas.

1 c. red onion, finely chopped
2 T. canola or olive oil
2 T. lemon juice
1/2 t. Dijon mustard
2 tomatoes, cut into wedges
14-1/2 oz. can cut green beans,
    drained

14-1/2 oz. can red kidney
    beans, drained and rinsed
1/4 c. sliced black olives,
    drained
1/4 c. bacon, crisply cooked
    and crumbled

In a large salad bowl, combine onion, oil, lemon juice and mustard.
Stir until well blended. Add tomatoes, green beans, kidney beans and
olives; toss gently. Cover and chill until serving time. Just before
serving, stir in bacon. Makes 6 to 8 servings.

Make it easy on yourself at the holidays! Instead of a sit-down
dinner, host an informal get-together. Set a favorite salad
or two alongside a selection of cold cuts, cheeses and
breads. Guests can help themselves.

Salads & Sides

Wilted Spinach Salad with Bacon

Carolyn Deckard
Bedford, IN

One of my favorite quick salads to make! It goes well with just about any other dishes you serve.

1 c. sliced mushrooms
1/3 c. green onions, sliced
1/3 c. Italian salad dressing
2 t. honey

6 c. fresh spinach, torn
2 T. bacon, crisply cooked
   and crumbled

In a skillet over medium heat, combine mushrooms, onions, salad dressing and honey. Bring to a boil; boil for one minute. Add spinach; toss for 15 to 30 seconds, just until spinach begins to wilt. Transfer to a large salad bowl; sprinkle with bacon. Serve immediately. Makes 4 servings.

Green Salad with Potatoes

Kathy Benkow
East Aurora, NY

This recipe has been handed down though the generations. It is the favorite side dish at our Sunday dinners and holiday celebrations. Smiles everywhere when it is brought to the table!

1/2 cucumber, peeled and
   thinly sliced
1 T. salt
3 small potatoes
1 onion, diced

1 head Boston or other leaf
   lettuce, torn
salt and pepper to taste
1/2 c. oil
1/4 c. cider vinegar

In a bowl, sprinkle cucumber slices with salt; set aside for one to 2 hours. In a saucepan, cover whole potatoes with water. Boil over medium heat until fork-tender, 10 to 15 minutes; drain. Peel potatoes; slice into a separate bowl. Rinse cucumber to remove most of the salt; drain and add to potatoes. Add onion and lettuce; mix gently. Season with salt and pepper; drizzle with oil to lightly cover and toss. Drizzle with vinegar; toss again. Makes 6 servings.

Strawberry & Romaine Salad

Jill Ball
Highland, UT

This is a wonderful salad to take to a holiday potluck. It looks like Christmas yet tastes like summer! Perfect on a cold winter's night.

1 c. sliced almonds
1 bunch fresh baby spinach

1 pt. strawberries, hulled
  and sliced

Make Raspberry Dressing; refrigerate. Lightly toast almonds in a dry frying pan over medium heat, stirring often. Remove to a bowl; set aside for several minutes. In a large salad bowl, toss spinach gently with strawberries; sprinkle with almonds. Serve immediately with Raspberry Dressing on the side, so guests may add as desired. Makes 6 servings.

Raspberry Dressing:

1/4 c. raspberry vinegar
1/3 c. canola oil
1/3 c. frozen raspberries, thawed
  and crumbled

1 t. sugar, honey or maple
  syrup
1/4 t. salt, or to taste

Combine all ingredients in a one-cup jar with a tight-fitting lid. Shake well to blend.

Sweet or spicy nuts make a tasty, crunchy salad garnish... just chop coarsely and sprinkle on!

Elise's Bacon & Broccoli Salad

Liz Plotnick-Snay
Gooseberry Patch

A former Gooseberry Patch employee used to make this salad for all our potlucks. It's wonderful!

1 bunch broccoli, cut into
   bite-size pieces
1 c. celery, chopped
1/2 c. red onion, chopped

6 to 8 slices bacon, crisply
   cooked and crumbled
1/2 c. raisins
1/3 c. sunflower seeds

Make Dressing ahead of time; set aside. Combine all ingredients in a large salad bowl; toss to mix. Cover and chill until serving time. Just before serving, drizzle with dressing. Toss to mix well. Serves 8 to 10.

Dressing:

3/4 c. mayonnaise
2 T. vinegar

1/4 c. sugar

Combine all ingredients in a small bowl; stir well until sugar dissolves.

A large clear glass bowl is a must for entertaining family & friends. Serve up a layered salad, a fruity punch or a sweet dessert trifle...even fill it with shiny glass ornaments to serve as a sparkly centerpiece.

Marinated Garden Salad

Amanda Bechtold
South Whitley, IN

*A very good salad recipe that's easily made ahead. Serve with
a weeknight meal, or make a double batch for a buffet.*

2 to 3 tomatoes, cubed
1 cucumber, peeled and cubed
1 green pepper, cut into strips
1 onion, sliced
1/2 c. sugar

1/4 c. vinegar
2 to 3 T. oil
2 T. mayonnaise-style salad
   dressing
1-1/2 T. soy sauce

Combine all vegetables in a salad bowl; set aside. In a separate bowl,
combine remaining ingredients. Whisk well and pour over vegetables;
toss to mix. Cover and chill overnight before serving. Makes 4 to
6 servings.

It's easy to mix & match...set a festive table with items you
already have! Green transferware serving bowls, sparkling white
porcelain dinner plates and ruby-red stemmed glasses combine
beautifully with each other and with Christmas dinnerware.

Yummy Corn Salad

Diane Paluch
Onsted, MI

This salad is a must at every family party. Every time someone tastes it for the first time, they have to have the recipe!

3 14-1/2 oz. cans yellow or
  yellow & white corn, drained
1 green pepper, chopped
1 bunch green onions, chopped
1 c. mayonnaise or mayonnaise-
  type salad dressing

8-oz. pkg. shredded sharp
  Cheddar cheese
9-oz. pkg. chili cheese corn
  chips, crushed

In a large salad bowl, combine corn, green pepper, onions, mayonnaise and cheese; mix well. Cover and refrigerate for at least 4 hours. Just before serving, add crushed corn chips; mix well. Serves 10.

Cranberry-Apple Salad

Susan Willie
Ridgecrest, NC

This recipe is quick & easy. Very tasty and festive!

2 c. whole-berry cranberry sauce
1 stalk celery, finely chopped

1 green apple, cored and diced
1/2 c. chopped walnuts

In a salad bowl, mix cranberry sauce, celery and apple. Cover and refrigerate. Stir in walnuts just before serving. Makes 6 servings.

Spoon servings of salad into individual leaves of radicchio lettuce. The cup-shaped red leaves can serve as both a salad bowl and a garnish.

Annie's Winter Couscous Bowl

Annelise Sophiea
Traverse City, MI

This recipe has become an instant winter classic in our household. The beautiful red, green and white colors make you feel right in the season. It's now a family favorite.

1/4 to 1/2 c. pine nuts
1 avocado, pitted, peeled
    and diced
2 t. lemon juice
1-1/2 c. water
1-1/2 c. couscous, uncooked
    and rinsed

1 cucumber, sliced
1 c. crumbled feta cheese
1/4 c. fresh cilantro, minced
seeds of 1 pomegranate
2 T. honey
1 t. cinnamon

Toast pine nuts in a dry skillet until golden; set aside. In a small bowl, mix together avocado and lemon juice; set aside. In a saucepan over high heat, bring water to a boil. Stir in couscous; cook until tender, about 20 minutes. Fluff couscous with a fork; transfer to a serving bowl. Add pine nuts, avocado mixture and remaining ingredients. Mix together thoroughly and serve. Serves 4 to 6.

Baffled by the best way to extract the juicy seeds from a pomegranate? Simply cut the pomegranate in half and tap with a wooden spoon over a bowl until the seeds fall out. Discard the bitter-tasting white membrane.

Salads & Sides

Super-Simple Italian Salad
Amy Thomason Hunt
Traphill, NC

A simple, tasty salad that goes well with lots of different mains.
Perfect with a party sandwich platter too.

16-oz. jar Italian giardiniera
    mix, drained and chopped
16-oz. pkg. mixed salad greens
4 tomatoes, cut into thin wedges
1 purple onion, diced

2 2-1/4 oz. cans sliced black
    olives, drained
grated Parmesan cheese and
    favorite salad dressing to
    taste

In a large salad bowl, combine giardiniera, salad greens, tomatoes,
onion and olives. Add cheese and salad dressing as desired; toss to
coat. Makes 6 to 8 servings.

Sweet Onion Herb Bread
Amy Butcher
Columbus, GA

I love whipping up a quick loaf of warm bread...it makes any meal
a little more special! Our Georgia sweet onions are perfect for this.

1-1/2 c. sweet onions,
    finely chopped
2 T. butter
3 c. buttermilk biscuit
    baking mix

1 egg, beaten
1 c. milk
1 t. dried thyme
1 t. dill weed

In a skillet over medium heat, sauté onions in butter until tender,
stirring constantly. Combine remaining ingredients in a large bowl;
add onion mixture. Stir just until blended and dry ingredients are
moistened. Spoon batter into a greased 9"x5" loaf pan. Bake at
350 degrees for 50 to 60 minutes. Turn out of pan; cool. Makes
one loaf.

To speed up dinner preparations, chop vegetables ahead of time.
Place in plastic zipping bags and store in the fridge...they'll be
ready to use when needed.

Holiday Red Cabbage Salad with Pine Nuts

Tyson Ann Trecannelli
Gettysburg, PA

This goes well with roast chicken, turkey or pork. It's an incredibly delicious, healthy salad that is sure to become a family favorite. Any leftovers will keep in the fridge for three to four days. We love it!

1 head red cabbage, quartered
1 carrot, peeled and shredded
1/2 c. sweetened dried
    cranberries, coarsely chopped
1/3 c. unsweetened shredded
    coconut

1/3 to 1/2 c. pine nuts
2 to 3 T. raspberry vinaigrette
2 T. agave nectar or honey
2 T. olive oil
1 T. cider vinegar
salt and pepper to taste

Finely shred cabbage in a food processor or with a sharp knife. In a large salad bowl, combine cabbage, carrot, cranberries, coconut and pine nuts; toss to mix. Combine remaining ingredients in a small bowl. Whisk together and pour over cabbage mixture; toss again. Serve immediately, or cover and refrigerate up to 2 hours before serving. Makes 10 to 12 servings.

A warm fruit compote is a delightful change from tossed salads. Simmer frozen sliced peaches, blueberries and raspberries together with a little honey, lemon juice and cinnamon, just until tender and syrupy.

Sharry's Apple Salad

Sharry Murawski
Oak Forest, IL

I like to make this salad because all the ingredients are available year 'round. The lime gives it such a refreshing taste.

2 Granny Smith apples, cored
   and diced
11-oz. can mandarin oranges,
   drained

1 c. seedless red grapes, halved
juice and zest of 1 lime
1-1/2 c. mini marshmallows
8-oz. container vanilla yogurt

In a large salad bowl, combine apples, oranges, grapes, lime juice and zest. Add marshmallows and yogurt; mix gently. Cover and refrigerate until ready to serve. Makes 4 to 6 servings.

Start a holiday journal. Decorate a blank book, then use it to note each year's special moments, meals enjoyed, guests welcomed and gifts given. You'll love looking back on these happy memories, and they'll help you in planning for future holidays!

Frozen Fruit Salad

Bootsie Dominick
Sandy Springs, GA

I love to serve this frozen fruit salad at Christmas luncheons with my friends. It is wonderful with chicken salad and cheese straws.

14-oz. can sweetened condensed
  milk
21-oz. can peach or cherry
  pie filling
15-oz. can mandarin oranges,
  drained
20-oz. can crushed pineapple,
  drained

2/3 c. chopped pecans or
  walnuts, toasted
8-oz. container frozen whipped
  topping, thawed
2 to 3 t. mayonnaise
Garnish: lettuce leaves

In a large bowl, combine condensed milk and pie filling; stir well. Add oranges, pineapple and nuts; gently fold in whipped topping. Lightly coat a 13"x9" baking pan with mayonnaise. Transfer mixture to pan; cover and freeze until solid. Remove from freezer 15 minutes before serving. Cut into squares; serve on lettuce leaves. Makes 12 to 15 servings.

Picture-perfect portions of Frozen Fruit Salad are handy for buffets or potlucks. Spoon the salad mixture into paper muffin liners and set in a baking pan. Chill until firm, then peel off liners.

Salads & Sides

Homestead Salad

Brenda Huey
Geneva, IN

This is a different combination and oh-so good! Excellent for holiday gatherings. For a smaller group, just halve the salad ingredients, then make the dressing, use half and save the rest for another time.

2 12-oz. pkgs. mixed salad
  greens
2 Red Delicious apples, cored
  and diced

1 c. cashews
1 c. baby Swiss cheese, cubed
1 c. sweetened dried cranberries

Make Poppy Seed Dressing; set aside. Combine all ingredients in a large salad bowl; mix gently. Pour Poppy Seed Dressing over salad and toss to coat. Makes 12 servings.

Poppy Seed Dressing:

3/4 c. sugar
1/3 c. cider vinegar
1 c. oil
2 T. dried, minced onion

1-1/2 t. poppy seed
1 t. seasoned salt
1 t. dry mustard

Combine all ingredients in a microwave-safe dish; blend well. Microwave on high for one minute, or until sugar dissolves. Cool.

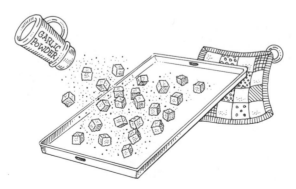

Make your own crispy croutons for soups and salads...so much tastier than the boxed kind. Toss cubes of day-old bread with olive oil and sprinkle with Italian seasoning or other dried herbs. Toast on a baking sheet at 400 degrees for 5 to 10 minutes, until golden.

Fruity Brown Rice Pilaf

Wendy Ball
Battle Creek, MI

This is a nice side dish for almost any occasion, especially Christmas.
It's lightly sweetened with dried fruits and just plain yummy.
Especially good with chicken and pork.

1 c. carrots, peeled and
   finely shredded
1 T. pine nuts
1 T. butter
1/2 c. quick-cooking brown
   rice, uncooked

1 c. unsweetened apple juice
3/4 c. water
6 dried apricots, finely chopped
2 T. golden raisins

Combine carrots, pine nuts and butter in a microwave-safe one-quart dish. Microwave on high for 2 minutes. Stir in uncooked rice, apple juice and water. Cover loosely with plastic wrap; microwave on high for 5 minutes, stirring with a fork after 3 minutes. Stir in apricots and raisins. Cover again; microwave on medium for 12 to 15 minutes, until liquid is absorbed and rice is tender. Fluff with a fork and serve. Makes 4 to 6 servings.

Simple Roasted Apples

Kathy Grashoff
Fort Wayne, IN

Perfect with pork chops! These tender apples make
the house smell wonderful while they're baking.

1/4 c. sugar
1/8 t. cinnamon

6 Gala apples, cored and cut
   into quarters

Combine sugar and cinnamon in a large bowl; add apples and toss to coat. Spread apples on an ungreased rimmed baking sheet in a single layer. Bake at 400 degrees for 30 to 35 minutes, tossing halfway through, until apples are tender but still firm. Serves 8.

Start a sweet new tradition at dinner. Hand out paper star cut-outs and have each person write down what they're happiest for since last Christmas.

Cranberry-Pear Relish

Dana Irish
Boise, ID

I am not usually a fan of cranberry relish, but a friend brought this to a cooking club dinner a few years ago, and I fell in love with it. It is different, and very, very good!

1/2 c. water
1-1/2 c. sugar
2 pears, peeled, cored and
   chopped

12-oz. pkg. fresh cranberries
1/2 t. nutmeg
1/2 t. allspice
4-inch cinnamon stick

Combine water and sugar in a saucepan. Bring to a boil over high heat; boil for 5 minutes. Add pears and cranberries. Cook and stir until cranberries pop. Stir in spices; add cinnamon stick. Cover and refrigerate 8 hours or overnight before serving. Serves 10.

Very Berry Cranberry Relish

Amy Mattock
Fairfax, VA

From Thanksgiving through Christmas, this recipe is a staple at all of our family get-togethers. No cooking needed!

2 14-oz. cans whole-berry
   cranberry sauce
20-oz. can crushed pineapple,
   drained

12-oz. pkg frozen raspberries,
   thawed and drained
12-oz. frozen strawberries,
   thawed and drained

In a large bowl, stir cranberry sauce until broken up. Stir in remaining ingredients. Cover and chill. Serves 10 to 12.

Don't toss out that little bit of leftover cranberry sauce! Purée it with balsamic vinaigrette to create a tangy salad dressing that's perfect over crisp greens and fruit.

Herb Garden Corn

Charity Miller
Tustin, MI

One of the tastiest ways to serve corn as a side...and it's so simple!

6 c. frozen corn
1/2 c. water
1/4 c. butter, cubed
1 T. dried parsley
1 t. salt

1/2 t. dill weed
1/4 t. garlic powder
1/4 t. Italian seasoning
1/8 t. dried thyme

In a large saucepan over medium heat, bring corn and water to a boil. Stir well. Reduce heat to medium-low. Cover and simmer for 4 to 6 minutes, until corn is tender. Drain; stir in butter and seasonings. Serves 8.

Easy Sesame Bread Sticks

Nancy Wise
Little Rock, AR

Serve these warm, cheesy bread sticks with your favorite soup or pasta meal.

11-oz. tube refrigerated
   bread sticks
1 egg, beaten
1 T. water

1 t. Dijon mustard
3/4 c. Asiago cheese, shredded
4-1/2 t. sesame seed
1/2 t. garlic powder

Unroll bread sticks; separate and set aside. In a small bowl, whisk together egg, water and mustard. In a separate bowl, combine remaining ingredients; mix well. Dip each bread stick into egg mixture; coat with cheese mixture. Twist each bread stick several times. Place on a lightly greased baking sheet, one inch apart. Firmly press down ends. Bake at 350 degrees for 14 to 19 minutes, until golden. Serve warm. Makes one dozen.

Wrap up hot bread sticks in a brightly colored bandanna... they'll stay toasty warm in the bread basket.

Sandra's Spinach Delight

Sandra Smith
Lancaster, CA

People who claim they don't like spinach change their mind after they've tried this dish! I've served this dish for the holidays for over 25 years. I began making it back when we hosted big dinner parties a couple times a year.

2 10-oz. pkgs. frozen chopped
   spinach, thawed and
   squeezed dry
16-oz. container cottage cheese
8-oz. pkg. shredded Cheddar
   cheese

1/2 c. butter, diced
6 eggs, beaten
salt and pepper to taste
1/4 c. all-purpose flour

Combine all ingredients in a large bowl, adding flour a little at a time. Stir just until mixed. Transfer to a buttered 2-quart casserole dish. Bake, uncovered, at 350 degrees for one hour, or until hot and bubbly. Serves 8 to 10.

Keep all of your family's favorite holiday storybooks in a basket by a cozy chair. Set aside one night as family night to read your favorites together.

Mom's Baked Mashed Potatoes *Susan Church*
Holly, MI

*These potatoes remind me of twice-baked potatoes in a casserole
dish...delicious! My mom started making them every holiday,
and I've carried on the tradition.*

3 lbs. baking potatoes, peeled
   and quartered
salt to taste
1-1/2 c. sour cream

5 T. butter, softened and divided
1-1/2 t. salt
1/4 t. pepper
1/4 c. dry bread crumbs

Bring a large saucepan of water to a boil over high heat. Add potatoes;
season generously with salt and cook until tender. Drain thoroughly;
transfer potatoes to a large bowl. Add sour cream, 4 tablespoons
butter, salt and pepper. Beat with an electric mixer on low speed until
blended. Beat on high speed until light and fluffy. Spoon mixture
lightly into a buttered 2-quart casserole dish. Cover and bake at
325 degrees for one hour. Melt remaining butter and toss with bread
crumbs; sprinkle over potatoes. Bake, uncovered, another 30 minutes.
Serves 8.

Traveling for the holidays? Have little ones leave Santa
a note with instructions telling him where you'll be
visiting the night before Christmas!

Salads & Sides

Sweet Potato Gratin

Jen Stout
Blandon, PA

This is a different and delicious twist on regular scalloped potatoes.

3 T. butter, divided
4 lbs. sweet potatoes, peeled
   and sliced crosswise,
   1/4-inch thick
3/4 c. grated Parmesan cheese

16-oz. container whipping
   cream
1 t. salt
1/2 t. pepper
Optional: 1/4 t. cayenne pepper

Brush a 13"x9" baking pan with one tablespoon butter. Arrange 1/3 of sweet potatoes in pan, overlapping slightly; sprinkle with 1/4 cup cheese. Repeat layering twice. In a small bowl, combine cream, salt, pepper and cayenne pepper, if using; spoon over potatoes. Dot with remaining butter. Cover with aluminum foil; bake at 400 degrees for 20 minutes. Uncover; bake until potatoes are tender and top is golden, 20 to 25 minutes. Serves 6 to 8.

Tasty Butternut Squash

Susan Brzozowski
Ellicott City, MD

My own twist on some recipes I've tried...we love it!
It's not only easy to prepare but also healthy.

1 butternut squash, peeled
   and seeded
2 T. extra virgin olive oil
1/2 t. coarse sea salt

1/2 c. water
2 T. butter, softened
1/2 t. dried thyme
coarse pepper to taste

Cut squash into 3/4-inch cubes; set aside. Heat olive oil in a large saucepan over medium-high heat. Add squash; sprinkle with salt. Cover and cook, stirring occasionally, until partially tender, about 8 minutes; reduce heat if squash begins to brown. Add water. Cover and simmer for about 15 minutes, stirring occasionally, until tender and water has nearly evaporated. Remove from heat. Add butter and seasonings; mash to desired consistency. Serves 6.

Serve a sweet potato dish in orange cups. Cut large oranges in half and scoop out the pulp with a grapefruit spoon.

Holiday Cornbread Dressing

Linda Trammell
Locust Grove, AR

*Every year for Thanksgiving and Christmas, my kids look forward to
my dressing made from fresh-baked skillet cornbread. It's a must!
While other side dishes have been exchanged for new ones, this one
will always be served at our home.*

2 eggs, beaten
10-3/4 oz. can cream of
   celery soup

1-1/2 t. dried sage
2 14-1/2 oz. cans chicken broth

Bake Skillet Cornbread ahead of time. Cool completely; slice and add to
a large plastic zipping bag. Crumble cornbread in bag; set aside. Whisk
together eggs, soup and sage in a bowl; pour over cornbread in bag
and mix well. Transfer to a greased 13"x9" baking pan; drizzle with
broth. Bake, uncovered, at 350 degrees for one hour, or until firm.
Serves 8.

Skillet Cornbread:

5 T. oil, divided
2 c. plus 1 t. cornmeal, divided
1-1/2 c. milk
1/2 c. onion, chopped

1 egg, beaten
2 T. sugar
1 T. dried sage

Preheat oven to 425 degrees. Pour 3 tablespoons oil into a cast-iron
skillet; dust skillet with one teaspoon cornmeal. Set in hot oven until
cornmeal is lightly golden; remove from oven. In a bowl, combine
remaining cornmeal, remaining oil and other ingredients; mix well.
Pour batter into hot skillet. Bake at 425 degrees for 45 minutes.

Slip Christmas cards into a vintage
napkin holder as they arrive in
your mailbox...share greetings
from friends and relatives over
dinner each day.

Buttery Orange-Glazed Carrots

Irene Robinson
Cincinnati, OH

Even people who don't like carrots love these!

2 c. carrots, peeled and sliced
   on the diagonal
2 T. honey
1 T. butter

1 t. orange zest
1/4 t. vanilla
salt to taste

Cover carrots with water in a saucepan. Bring to a boil over medium-high heat; simmer for 8 minutes, or until carrots are crisp-tender. Drain; return to saucepan. Add remaining ingredients. Bring to a boil; cook and stir until carrots are glazed. Serves 4.

Lemon Pilaf

Shirley Howie
Foxboro, MA

The lemon gives this dish a bright, fresh taste which goes very well with baked chicken or fish.

1 c. celery, sliced
1 c. green onions, sliced
2 T. butter, melted
3 c. hot cooked rice

1 T. lemon zest
1 t. salt
1/4 t. pepper

In a large saucepan over medium heat, sauté celery and onions in butter until soft and golden. Add cooked rice, lemon zest, salt and pepper; toss to blend well. Cook and stir over low heat for one to 2 minutes, until heated through. Makes 6 servings.

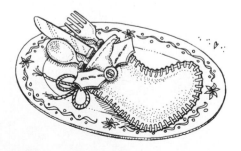

Tuck silverware into plush red
mini Christmas stockings
to lay on each guest's plate...
so festive!

Quick & Easy Macaroni & Cheese Casserole

Angela Bowden Iery
Vanceburg, KY

My mom and granny just love macaroni & cheese. When this particular recipe is made, you'd better grab some before it's all gone! The cottage cheese does sound unusual, but makes it so delicious. I love to make it for dinner and get-togethers. My friends love it too and are surprised how easy the recipe is. I believe it will become your favorite mac & cheese recipe too.

2 c. elbow macaroni, uncooked
1/2 c. butter
16-oz. container small-curd cottage cheese
salt and pepper to taste
2-1/2 c. boiling water
8-oz. pkg. shredded Cheddar cheese

Spread uncooked macaroni in a buttered 13"x9" glass baking pan. Slice butter over macaroni. Spread cottage cheese on top. Sprinkle with salt and pepper. Pour boiling water over top. Cover with Cheddar cheese. Bake at 350 degrees for one hour, or until bubbly and macaroni is tender. Makes 6 to 8 servings.

For somehow, not only at Christmas,
but all the year through,
The joy that you give to others
is the joy that comes back to you.

–Margaret Sangster

Salads & Sides

No-Fail Fettuccine Alfredo

Michelle Powell
Valley, AL

The easy no-cook sauce can be made ahead of time and
refrigerated to top pasta or vegetables for a quick supper side.

16-oz. pkg. fettuccine pasta,
   uncooked
1/2 c. butter, softened
1/4 c. whipping cream

1/2 c. grated Parmesan cheese
salt and pepper to taste
Optional: additional Parmesan
   cheese

Cook pasta according to package directions; drain. Meanwhile, beat
butter until fluffy; blend in cream a little at a time. Blend in cheese.
Toss hot pasta with butter mixture; season with salt and pepper. Serve
with additional cheese, if desired. Serves 8.

Sweet-and-Sour Green Beans

Paula James
Edgar Springs, MO

This recipe was originally my sister's, and it's one of my favorites.
Everyone I have made these beans for loves them...I often get calls
from family & friends wanting the recipe.

4 slices bacon, cut into
   1-inch pieces
2 14-1/2 oz. cans cut
   green beans

1/2 c. onion, chopped
1/3 c. brown sugar, packed
1/3 c. vinegar
salt and pepper to taste

In a deep skillet over medium heat, cook bacon until crisp; drain.
Drain half the liquid from beans; add beans to skillet. Stir in remaining
ingredients. Simmer over low heat for about 45 minutes, until some of
the liquid has evaporated. Serves 6 to 8.

Ring out a holiday greeting to
visitors...hang a string of sleigh bells
on the front door.

Cheesy Potato Puffs

Mandy Schafer
Monroeville, OH

Always requested...there are rarely any left!

10-3/4 oz. can cream of
    onion soup
8-oz. container sour cream
1/4 c. butter, melted
1/2 onion, chopped
1/4 t. seasoning salt

1/4 t. pepper
32-oz. pkg. frozen potato puffs
3 c. shredded Cheddar cheese
paprika and dried chives to taste
1 c. corn flake cereal, crushed

In a large bowl, combine soup, sour cream, butter, onion, salt and pepper; mix well. Add potato puffs and cheese; toss gently to mix well. Transfer to a 13"x9" baking pan sprayed with non-stick spray. Sprinkle lightly with paprika and chives. Bake, uncovered, at 350 degrees for 45 minutes. Top with corn flakes; bake an additional 15 minutes, or until bubbly and golden. Serves 8 to 10.

In need of a tree skirt? A jolly vintage Christmas tablecloth
with its brightly colored images of Santas, elves or carolers
is easily wrapped around the tree for a bit of
old-fashioned holiday fun.

Salads & Sides

Hand-Me-Down Broccoli Soufflé

Lacey Wahl
Port Townsend, WA

This recipe has been handed down through my family,
and it's a must at any holiday.

2 10-oz. pkgs frozen chopped
   broccoli, thawed and drained
10-3/4 oz. can cream of
   mushroom soup
2 eggs, beaten
1 c. mayonnaise

1 c. shredded Cheddar cheese
1/2 c. onion, finely chopped
Garnish: additional cheese
   and/or canned French fried
   onions

Combine all ingredients except garnish in a lightly greased 2-quart casserole dish. Mix well. Bake, uncovered, at 350 degrees for about 30 minutes. Garnish as desired; return to oven for 5 minutes. Serves 6 to 8.

Turn a white cotton tablecloth into a family memento. Using a permanent marker, ask each family member (friends too!) to write a holiday message, draw a picture and sign their names along with the year. Younger children can trace around their hands...sweet!

Southwest Corn Strata

Sherry Rhoads
Grove, OK

I have been making this dish for 20 years...our Thanksgiving and Christmas dinners would not be the same without it! A friend shared the recipe with me in the early 1990s.

1 loaf French or Italian bread,
    ends trimmed
3 T. butter, softened
2 15-oz. cans corn, drained
14-3/4 oz. can creamed corn
4-oz. jar diced pimentos, drained
3 10-oz. cans whole green
    chiles, drained and
    1/4 c. liquid reserved

salt and pepper to taste
3/4 c. onion, chopped
1/3 c. fresh cilantro, chopped
8-oz. pkg. shredded Monterey
    Jack cheese, divided
6 eggs, beaten
1 c. milk

Spray a 13"x9" baking pan with non-stick vegetable spray; set aside. Cut loaf into 16 slices; spread all slices with butter on both sides. Arrange 8 slices in bottom of pan; set aside. In a bowl, combine corn, creamed corn, pimentos and reserved liquid from chiles. Spoon half of mixture over bread in pan; season with salt and pepper. Slice chiles into strips; arrange half of chile strips over corn mixture. Sprinkle onion, cilantro and one cup cheese evenly over top. Arrange remaining bread slices on top. Repeat layering with remaining corn mixture, chiles and cheese. In a bowl, beat together eggs and milk; season with salt and pepper. Pour over top; spread remaining cheese on top. Bake, uncovered, at 350 degrees for 55 to 60 minutes, until hot and bubbly. Serves 10.

For a cheery winter welcome, fill a child's wagon with poinsettias and vintage ornaments and place by the front door.

Salads & Sides

Favorite Roasted Vegetables

Kathy Collins
Brookfield, CT

My family loves vegetables roasted this way...
they're flavorful and tender.

2 T. olive oil
2 to 3 cloves garlic, minced
1 T. fresh thyme, snipped
1/2 t. salt
1/2 t. pepper
1 lb. potatoes, quartered

1 onion, quartered
3 carrots, cut into 1-inch
  sections
3 stalks celery, cut into
  1 inch sections

Preheat oven to 425 degrees. Combine oil and garlic in a shallow 13"x9" baking pan. Place pan in oven for 2 minutes, or until garlic sizzles; stir in seasonings. Add vegetables to pan; stir to coat and arrange in a single layer. Cover and bake at 425 degrees for 30 minutes, or until vegetables are tender. Serves 6.

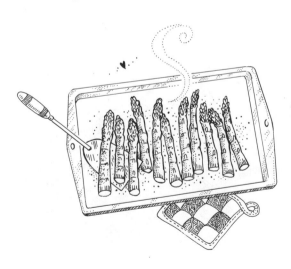

Slow-roasted vegetables are flavorful, nutritious and so versatile... try roasting asparagus, butternut squash and sweet peppers, to name a few more. Serve them warm as a side dish, or cool, spoon over crisp greens and drizzle with vinaigrette dressing for a tasty salad. They can even be tossed with thin spaghetti and crumbled feta cheese for a hearty meatless main dish. Yum!

Southern Stir-Fried Cabbage

Tina Butler
Royse City, TX

This is our favorite cabbage dish to serve with black-eyed peas on New Year's Day. It pairs perfectly with baked ham, smoked pork chops or smoked sausage.

3 to 4 slices bacon, coarsely
    chopped
1/4 c. oil
1 t. salt, or to taste
1 t. pepper

1 head cabbage, sliced or cubed
1/2 c. onion, chopped
1/2 c. water
1/8 t. sugar
2 cubes beef bouillon, crushed

Combine bacon and oil in a large saucepan over medium heat. Cook for about 5 minutes, or until bacon is crisp. Add remaining ingredients to pan. Cook and stir over medium heat until cabbage is tender-crisp, about 10 to 15 minutes. Makes 8 servings.

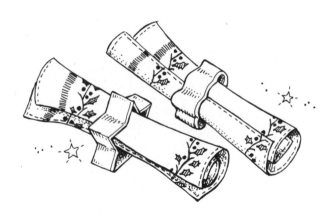

Cookie cutters make clever napkin rings...just slip the rolled-up napkin through the center. With a different shape for each person, it's easy to know whose napkin is whose.

Salads & Sides

Aunt Norma's Hoppin' John

Pamela Mueri
Lincoln, NE

This recipe was made famous in our family by our Aunt Norma, the fun, exciting, sloppy-kissing aunt who always makes us light up inside. She loves to cook and will teach you how to make anything you desire. With each visit she makes something more amazing than the last. I like to add a little onion salt and cumin to spice it up a bit, but really, it's perfect the way it is.

1 lb. bacon	2-1/2 c. water
2 T. butter	1/4 t. garlic salt
1 onion, chopped	1/4 t. salt, or to taste
2 14-oz. cans black-eyed peas	1-1/2 t. pepper, or to taste
2 c. long-cooking rice, uncooked	Optional: chopped fresh parsley

In a large skillet over medium heat, cook bacon until crisp; drain and set aside. In the same skillet, melt butter. Add onion; sauté until onion is translucent but still has some crunch. Add peas with liquid and water; stir in uncooked rice. Cover and simmer for 30 to 40 minutes, until rice is tender; add seasonings. Add crumbled bacon; mix thoroughly. Sprinkle with parsley, if desired. Serves 6.

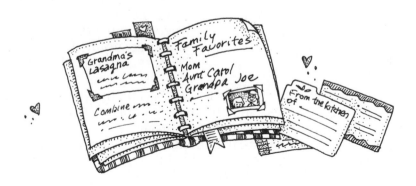

Invite family & friends to share tried & true favorites and create a holiday recipe scrapbook...a great gift for a new cook in the family.

Home-Baked Beans

Linda Johnston
Madison Heights, MI

I got this recipe from my late mother-in-law. It is now one of my most-requested dishes to bring to dinners with my friends who have become like another family to me.

42-oz. can Great Northern
    beans, partially drained
1/2 c. onion, chopped
1/2 c. brown sugar, packed
3 to 5 T. molasses

1/2 t. ground ginger
1 t. dry mustard
salt and pepper to taste
6 slices bacon

Combine all ingredients except bacon in a greased 2-1/2 quart casserole dish. Arrange bacon slices on top. Bake, uncovered, at 375 degrees until bubbly and bacon is crisp, about 1-1/2 hours. Serves 8 to 10.

Cheesy Green Bean Bake

Diane Price
Nappanee, IN

This is my all-time favorite side dish to make... always requested for family gatherings. Very easy and you will get many compliments.

1/2 lb. bacon, diced
1 T. onion, finely chopped
10-3/4 oz. can cream of
    mushroom soup
salt to taste

2 14-1/2 oz. cans cut green
    beans, drained
4-oz. can mushroom stems &
    pieces, drained
1 c. shredded Cheddar cheese

In a large skillet over medium heat, cook bacon until crisp. Set bacon aside, reserving drippings. Add onion; cook until golden. Stir in soup and salt. Add beans; stir until coated. Transfer mixture to a lightly greased shallow 8"x8" baking pan. Sprinkle with mushrooms and cheese; top with crumbled bacon. Bake, uncovered, at 350 degrees for 30 minutes. Makes 8 servings.

Toss a bundle of cinnamon sticks or orange peel into
a crackling fire for a delightful fragrance.

FAMILY-PLEASING
Holiday Meals

3-Pasta Casserole

Laura Davis
Abilene, KS

I love to make this casserole for my family & friends as a "just because" gift. It's a great way to fill in one night, not having to cook...always appreciated! If you don't have all these kinds of pasta, it's fine to use 3 cups of one kind...but the mixed-up shapes are fun!

1 c. penne pasta, uncooked
1 c. rotini pasta, uncooked
1 c. bowtie pasta, uncooked
3-oz. pkg. sliced pepperoni, divided
1 c. green pepper, diced and divided
1 c. red pepper, diced and divided

24-oz. jar chunky garden pasta sauce, divided
8-oz. pkg. shredded mozzarella cheese, divided
Garnish: grated Parmesan cheese

Cook all 3 pastas together according to package directions, just until tender; drain. Transfer half of cooked pasta to a buttered 3-quart casserole dish. Layer with half of pepperoni, 1/4 cup green pepper, 1/4 cup red pepper, half of pasta sauce and half of mozzarella cheese. Repeat layering with remaining ingredients; sprinkle with Parmesan cheese. Bake, uncovered, at 350 degrees for 20 minutes, or until bubbly and cheese melts. Makes 6 to 8 servings.

A big dish of your favorite pasta is a delightful, easy meal for a casual get-together with friends. Just add warm garlic bread, a big tossed salad and plenty of paper napkins!

Christmas Eve Ravioli

Susan Jacobs
Vista, CA

We have a potluck on Christmas Eve every year. I wanted something quick to fix while wrapping gifts, and this is what I came up with. It cooks in a slow cooker, freeing me up to do all the other things I do for Christmas Eve.

25-oz. jar 4-cheese marinara
   sauce
15-oz. can tomato sauce
1 zucchini, diced
7-oz. can mushroom stems &
   pieces, drained

4-oz. can diced green chiles
18-oz. pkg. refrigerated spinach
   & cheese ravioli
Garnish: grated Parmesan
   cheese

Turn a 4-quart slow cooker to high setting; let warm for several minutes. Add sauces; stir to mix. Cover and cook on high setting for 2 hours. Stir in zucchini; cover and cook for one hour. Add mushrooms, chiles and ravioli; stir gently. Cover and cook for one more hour, or until zucchini and ravioli are tender. Allow guests to serve themselves, topping with Parmesan cheese. Serves 5 to 6.

Decadent Cheesy Garlic Bread

Jessica Kraus
Delaware, OH

The most over-the-top garlic bread you will ever taste. It turns any pasta meal into a feast!

1/4 c. butter, softened
1 c. mayonnaise
8-oz. pkg. shredded 3-cheese
   blend
2 cloves garlic, minced

1 c. green onions, diced and
   divided
1 loaf French or Italian bread,
   halved lengthwise

In a bowl, combine butter, mayonnaise, cheese, garlic and 3/4 cup onions. Stir until well combined. Spread mixture over cut sides of bread; place bread on a broiler pan. Bake at 350 degrees for 7 minutes. Place pan under broiler and broil just until golden, about 3 minutes. Slice bread; top with remaining onions. Serves 10.

Holiday Ham & Cheese Bake

Joyceann Dreibelbis
Wooster, OH

A quick & easy dish that everyone enjoys for either brunch or dinner.
The diced red and green peppers give it a festive appeal.

4 c. frozen diced potatoes
3 c. broccoli flowerets, cut into
   bite-size pieces
1 c. green pepper, diced
1 c. red pepper, diced
1/2 c. onion, chopped
1-1/2 c. cooked ham, diced

8-oz. pkg. shredded mild
   Cheddar cheese, divided
4 eggs, beaten
2/3 c. milk
1/2 t. salt
1/2 t. pepper

Combine potatoes, broccoli, peppers, onion and ham in a large bowl; toss well. Arrange half of potato mixture in an 8"x8" glass baking pan coated with non-stick vegetable spray. Top with one cup cheese, remaining potato mixture and remaining cheese; set aside. In a separate bowl, whisk eggs with milk, salt and pepper; pour evenly over potato mixture. Bake, uncovered, at 375 degrees for 40 minutes, or until bubbly and cheese is melted. Let stand 5 minutes before serving. Serves 6.

Get ready to celebrate! Early in December, press the table linens and polish the silver. Later, as holiday meals and parties are being prepared, you can relax knowing these tasks are already done.

Salisbury Meatballs

Shirley Howie
Foxboro, MA

This comfort food favorite is a quick take on Salisbury steak...
it can be made in just over 30 minutes. I like to serve it in
bowls, ladled over noodles or rice. A delicious one-dish meal!

12-oz. pkg. frozen Italian-style
   meatballs
2 T. olive oil
1/2 c. onion, sliced
1 T. all-purpose flour
1-1/2 c. chicken or beef broth

2 T. tomato paste
1/2 t. Dijon mustard
2 T. Worcestershire sauce
salt and pepper to taste
3 c. cooked egg noodles or rice

Place frozen meatballs on a lightly greased rimmed baking sheet. Bake at 350 degrees for 30 minutes. Meanwhile, heat oil in a skillet over medium heat. Add onion; cook until lightly golden, about 4 minutes. Sprinkle onion with flour; stir to coat and cook another 2 minutes. Stir in remaining ingredients except noodles or rice. Bring to a simmer; cook about 10 minutes. Add baked meatballs to the sauce in skillet; stir to coat. Serve meatballs and sauce over cooked egg noodles or rice. Makes 4 servings.

Take the family to a local tree farm and cut your own Christmas tree! Afterwards, warm up with mugs of hot cocoa. You'll be creating sweet memories!

Saturday Noodle Bake

Kathie Boglovits
Kernersville, NC

My grandmother used to make this for me, and it has always been one of my favorites. After I got married, it continued to be a quick dinner go-to and is now a favorite of my stepson.

1 lb. ground beef
1/2 c. onion, chopped
2 10-3/4 oz. cans tomato soup
3-oz. pkg. cream cheese, cubed

Optional: 1 T. sugar
1 T. Worcestershire sauce
6-oz. pkg. wide egg noodles,
  uncooked

In a skillet over medium heat, brown beef and onion; drain. Add remaining ingredients except noodles. Cook and stir until well combined and cheese is melted. Simmer for 15 minutes, stirring occasionally. While beef mixture is simmering, cook noodles according to package directions; drain. Transfer noodles to a greased 13"x9" baking pan. Top with beef mixture; stir gently. Bake, uncovered, at 350 degrees for 15 minutes, or until heated through. Serves 4 to 6.

Garlic & Herb Crescents

Jenny Wright
Carneys Point, NJ

This is a super-easy recipe that my family has been making for years. Holiday meals just wouldn't be the same without these!

8-oz. tube refrigerated crescent
  rolls

8-oz. container garlic & herb
  cheese spread

Separate crescent rolls. Cut each roll lengthwise, to make 16 small triangles. Spread one teaspoon cheese on each roll. Roll up, starting at the wider edge. Place rolls on an ungreased baking sheet. Bake at 375 degrees for 11 to 13 minutes, until golden. Makes 16 small rolls.

Bring a bit of retro to the holiday kitchen...tie on a vintage Christmas apron!

Southern Sausage & Pintos

Tammy Rogers
Gordonsville, VA

I always keep the ingredients for this recipe on hand for those evenings when I need a quick and delicious, practically effortless dinner. Delicious served with a crisp salad and warm cornbread.

7-oz. pkg. frozen brown & serve
   pork sausage links
1 c. onion, chopped

1 green pepper, chopped
2 15-oz. cans pinto beans
8-oz. can tomato sauce

In a skillet, cook sausage links according to package directions, adding onion and pepper to skillet. Cut each sausage link into thirds; stir in beans and tomato sauce. Simmer over low heat until onion and pepper are tender, about 20 minutes. Makes 6 to 8 servings.

Running to the window, he opened it, and put out his head.
Golden sunlight; heavenly sky; sweet fresh air; merry bells...
oh glorious! glorious! Christmas Day!

–Charles Dickens

Creamy Baked Chicken & Mushrooms

Tanya Schroeder
Cincinnati, OH

Pure comfort food! I make this dish in the winter for my family. It always goes so quickly, and we fight over each little crumb of bacon.

4 slices bacon
4 boneless, skinless chicken
   breasts
1 t. salt
1/4 t. pepper
3 T. butter
3 T. all-purpose flour
1/2 c. onion, diced

1/2 lb. baby bella mushrooms,
   sliced
14-oz. can chicken broth
4.6-oz. container garlic & herb
   cheese spread
2 to 3 roma tomatoes, chopped
cooked spaghetti

In a large skillet over medium heat, cook bacon until crisp. Remove bacon to a plate; set aside. Reserving 2 tablespoons drippings, wipe skillet clean. Season chicken with salt and pepper; add to drippings and cook over medium heat until golden on both sides. Remove chicken to a greased 2-quart casserole dish; set aside. Melt butter in skillet; stir in flour. Add onion and mushrooms; cook for about one minute. Stir in chicken broth and cheese spread. Continue to stir until smooth. Pour sauce over chicken in casserole dish; sprinkle with tomatoes and crumbled bacon. Bake, uncovered, at 350 degrees for 20 to 25 minutes. Serve chicken and sauce over cooked spaghetti. Makes 4 servings.

Streamline your holiday plans...just ask your family what traditions they cherish the most, including favorite cookies and other festive foods. You can focus on tried & true activities and free up time to try something new.

Winner Winner Chicken Dinner

*Jewel Sharpe
Raleigh, NC*

A complete baked chicken dinner in a 13"x9" pan...easy-peasy!

4 to 6 boneless, skinless chicken
    breasts, cut in half
2 14-1/2 oz. cans green beans,
    drained

6 redskin potatoes, halved
0.7-oz. pkg. zesty Italian
    dressing mix
1/2 c. butter, melted

Arrange chicken down the center of a lightly greased 13"x9" baking pan. Add green beans on one side of chicken; add potatoes on the other side. Sprinkle dressing mix over all. Drizzle melted butter over all. Cover with aluminum foil. Bake at 350 degrees for one hour. Serves 4 to 6.

Red Pepper Jelly Chicken

*Barb Rudyk
Alberta, Canada*

*A very quick & easy recipe...just a few ingredients and great
flavor. A tasty way to enjoy that jar of red pepper jelly
in your Christmas gift basket!*

2 lbs. chicken drumsticks
1/3 c. red pepper jelly

1/3 c. Dijon mustard
1/3 c. honey

Arrange drumsticks in a greased 13"x9" baking pan; set aside. In a small saucepan over low heat, combine remaining ingredients. Cook and stir until well blended; spoon mixture over chicken. Bake, uncovered, at 350 degrees for one to 1-1/2 hours. Serves 6.

A no-cook appetizer that's ready in moments! Unwrap a log of herbed goat cheese and roll it in chopped fresh parsley. Place it on a serving dish and surround with crisp crackers. Handy when you're putting the finishing touches on dinner.

Saucy Beef Brisket

Geraldine Saucier
Albuquerque, NM

This is a family favorite for Christmas Eve dinner. It's a great
slow-cooker recipe for busy days or whenever you just
want something delicious and easy to prepare.

4-1/2 to 5-lb. beef brisket,
   cut in half and fat trimmed
1/2 c. barbecue sauce
1/4 c. chili sauce
1/4 c. soy sauce
2 T. Worcestershire sauce

2 t. smoke-flavored cooking
   sauce
1 t. hot pepper sauce
Optional: additional barbecue
   sauce

Place each brisket half on a large piece of aluminum foil; set aside.
Combine all sauces in a bowl; mix well. Spoon half of sauce mixture
over each half of brisket. Wrap each brisket in foil, making 2 sealed
packages; place in a 6-quart slow cooker. Cover and cook on low
setting for 6 hours. Let stand for 10 minutes before slicing. Serve with
extra barbecue sauce, if desired. Serves 6 to 8.

Host a Christmas Eve buffet without the fuss. Split the meal
into courses and let guests choose a course to bring...spend
less time in the kitchen and more with family & friends!

Easy Beef & Veggie Skillet

Shirley Howie
Foxboro, MA

This is a healthy and delicious weeknight meal that comes together in a flash! The herbs in the stuffing mix give it a wonderful flavor. I make this dish often.

1 lb. lean ground beef
3/4 c. onion, chopped
14-1/2 oz. can stewed tomatoes
2 zucchini, quartered lengthwise
   and sliced

2 c. herb-seasoned cubed
   stuffing mix
2 T. grated Parmesan cheese
Optional: additional grated
   Parmesan cheese

In a large skillet over medium-high heat, cook beef and onion until well browned, stirring to separate beef. Drain very well. Add tomatoes with juice and zucchini; bring to a boil. Reduce heat to low; cover and cook for 5 minutes, or until zucchini is tender. Remove from heat. Add stuffing mix and cheese to skillet; mix lightly. Cover and let stand 5 minutes. Serve with additional cheese, if desired. Makes 4 servings.

Whip up a snowflake scene for a window...simply pair white or silver peel & stick bows along a strand of white yarn. Make several and hang in the window with thumb tacks...splendid!

Slow-Cooked Turkey Breast & Gravy

Jennie Gist
Gooseberry Patch

This recipe saves me so much time and effort on Christmas Day! I pop the turkey in the slow cooker early in the morning, then we all open our gifts and enjoy the afternoon together before sitting down to our turkey dinner. Pass the cranberry sauce, please!

4-lb. bone-in turkey breast,
   thawed if frozen

1-oz. pkg. onion soup mix
3 T. butter, sliced

Pat turkey dry with paper towels; rub soup mix all over turkey. Add butter to a 6-quart slow cooker; place turkey on top. Cover and cook on low setting for 7 hours, or until a meat thermometer inserted in the center reads 165 degrees. Remove turkey to a platter, reserving drippings in slow cooker. Cover turkey lightly with aluminum foil and let stand while making Turkey Gravy. Slice turkey; serve with gravy. Serves 6.

Turkey Gravy:

reserved turkey drippings
2 T. cornstarch

2 T. cold water
salt and pepper to taste

Strain drippings from slow cooker into a saucepan over medium heat; heat through. Mix cornstarch and water in a small bowl; slowly whisk into drippings. Cook and whisk for about 5 minutes, until thickened and smooth. Season with salt and pepper.

For dark, rich-looking gravy, add a spoonful or two of brewed coffee. It will add color to pale gravy but won't affect the flavor.

Holiday Turkey Casserole

Janis Parr
Ontario, Canada

This is a great way to enjoy the leftover turkey from Christmas dinner. This casserole can be assembled a day ahead, refrigerated and then baked when ready to serve, making it so convenient at the busiest time of the year.

1-1/2 c. celery, chopped
3/4 c. onion, minced
6 T. butter, sliced
6 T. all-purpose flour
1/2 t. salt
1/2 t. pepper
3 c. milk

10-3/4 oz. can cream of
    mushroom soup
6 T. cooking sherry or chicken
    broth
1/2 t. dried basil
4 c. roast turkey, cubed
1 c. shredded Cheddar cheese

In a large saucepan over medium-low heat, sauté celery and onion in butter until just tender. Stir in flour, salt and pepper. Add milk and cook until thickened, stirring constantly. Stir in soup, sherry or broth and basil; fold in turkey. Transfer to a buttered 2-quart casserole dish; top with cheese. Cover and refrigerate. To serve, uncover and bake 350 degrees for one hour, or until bubbly and cheese is melted. Makes 6 to 8 servings.

Do you have lots of leftover turkey? It freezes well for up to 3 months. Cut turkey into bite-size pieces, place in plastic freezer bags and pop in the freezer...ready to stir into hearty casseroles and soups whenever you are.

Pasta Shell Tacos

Jayne O'Brien
Groveland, IL

*In my family, we all enjoy these Mexican-flavored stuffed shells.
Sometimes I will double or triple the recipe then refrigerate after the
taco sauce step. Then when the children come to visit, they can bake
as many as they like, anytime they like.*

18 jumbo pasta shells, uncooked
2 T. butter, melted
1-1/4 lbs. ground beef
3-oz. pkg. cream cheese with
    chives, softened
1 t. chili powder

1 t. salt
1 c. smooth taco sauce
1 c. shredded Cheddar cheese
1 c. shredded Monterey jack
    cheese
1-1/2 c. tortilla chips, crushed

Cook pasta shells according to package directions, just until tender.
Drain; toss with melted butter and set aside. Meanwhile, cook beef
in a large skillet over medium heat until browned and crumbled; drain.
Reduce heat to low. Stir in cream cheese and seasonings; simmer for
5 minutes. Spoon beef mixture into shells. Arrange filled shells in a
lightly greased 13"x9" baking pan. Spoon some taco sauce into each
shell. Cover with aluminum foil. Bake at 350 degrees for 15 minutes.
Uncover; top shells with shredded cheese and crushed chips. Bake
another 10 to 15 minutes, until hot and bubbly. Serves 6.

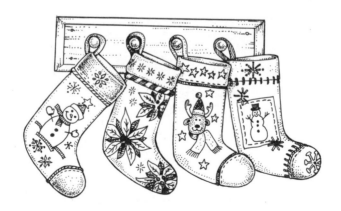

No mantel for hanging stockings? Mount Shaker pegs on
a wooden board, one for each member of the family!

Easiest-Ever Nachos

Wanda Wilson
Hamilton, GA

My daughter-in-law has devised quick, tasty meals for her family that she can have on the table in 30 minutes or less after she arrives home from work. I have plenty of time to cook, but why work harder than necessary when something tastes this great?

1 lb. ground beef
1/2 c. onion, chopped
15-1/2 oz. can black beans,
    drained
1/2 to 2/3 c. salsa
8-oz. Mexican pasteurized
    process cheese, cubed

1 to 2 t. milk
9-oz. pkg. tortilla chips
Garnish: chopped black olives,
    diced green chiles,
    sour cream

Brown beef and onion in a skillet over medium heat; drain. Add beans and salsa; stir and heat through. Place cubed cheese in a microwave-safe dish. Cover and microwave at 30-second intervals until melted, adding milk as needed; stir until smooth. To serve, cover 4 dinner plates with tortilla chips. Ladle beef sauce over chips; top with melted cheese and toppings as desired. Serves 4.

Speed up prep time on ground beef recipes. Brown several pounds of beef, adding chopped onions if you like. Divide into one-pound portions in large plastic freezer bags and flatten to freeze. The packages will thaw quickly when needed.

Aunt Flora's Juicyburgers

Theresa Wehmeyer
Rosebud, MO

Each year after Christmas Eve worship, my husband's whole family would gather at Aunt Flora and Uncle Art's home. There was a bounty of delicious food and their tiny home, including the basement, was filled with family. These sandwiches were always served. I am thankful Aunt Flora shared the recipe with me.

3 lbs. ground beef
1/2 onion, finely diced
14-oz. bottle catsup
1/4 t. Worcestershire sauce

1 T. lemon juice
2 T. brown sugar, packed
3/4 t. dry mustard
18 to 20 sandwich buns, split

Brown beef and onion in a large skillet over medium heat; drain. Add remaining ingredients except buns. Reduce heat to low; simmer for 10 to 15 minutes to combine flavors. To serve, spoon onto buns. Serves 18 to 20.

Aunt Eunice's Sloppy Joes

Pam Ludwig
Imboden, AR

This is an easy-peasy recipe. My Aunt Eunice used to have a huge batch of this simmering every Christmas Eve for all her family, and everyone loved her Sloppy Joes. I'm so thankful that she passed it down to me.

1 lb. ground beef
1/2 c. onion, chopped
1 green pepper, chopped
2 10-3/4 oz. cans tomato soup

2 T. Worcestershire sauce
3 T. pasteurized process cheese
   sauce
4 sandwich buns, split

Brown beef, onion and green pepper in a skillet over medium heat; drain. Stir in soup and sauces; reduce heat to low. Simmer for about 20 minutes. To serve, spoon onto buns. Serves 4.

Serve up tasty sandwich fillings piping-hot to a crowd! After cooking, transfer to a slow cooker set on low.

Poppy Seed Sandwiches

Valerie Shockley
Portland, TN

Christmas Eve at our house always meant looking at Christmas lights, The Night Before Christmas, trying to get a peek at Santa, hot chocolate, sparkling grape juice in the fancy glasses...and these sandwiches. They are warm melty goodness! Best of all, they can be prepared ahead of time, then baked just before mealtime.

1 c. butter, softened
2 T. mustard
2 T. poppy seed
15 to 16 kaiser rolls or hard
    rolls, split

15 to 16 slices deli ham
15 to 16 slices Muenster
    cheese

Blend butter, mustard and poppy seed in a bowl. Spread on cut sides of rolls. Fill each roll with one slice ham and one slice cheese; wrap in aluminum foil. At this point, sandwiches may be frozen. Place on a baking sheet and bake at 350 degrees for 25 minutes. If frozen, bake at 350 degrees for 30 to 45 minutes. Makes 15 to 16 servings.

Souperburgers

Eileen Bennett
Jenison, MI

Cookie baking day and no time to cook? Make up a batch of these sandwiches, and dinner will be ready when you are. Our family has been making them for three generations. Grandma B (that's me) began the tradition in the 1960s. An all-time favorite!

1 lb. ground beef
3/4 c. onion, chopped
10-3/4 oz. can chicken gumbo
    soup
1/4 c. catsup

3 T. brown sugar, packed
seasoned salt and seasoned
    pepper to taste
6 buns, split, toasted and
    buttered

In a skillet over medium heat, brown beef and onion; drain. Stir in remaining ingredients except buns. Simmer for 5 to 10 minutes to blend flavors, stirring occasionally. To serve, spoon onto buns. Serves 6.

Sour Cream Enchiladas

Pamela Bennett
Whittier, CA

This is a super-easy meal to toss together. It's a recipe that I have been making not only for my family, but whenever I have a large crowd to cook for. Everyone loves it as it isn't spicy. Canned chicken speeds it up, but you can use 4 to 5 cooked, shredded chicken breasts if you like. Just add a chopped salad with lime dressing for a delicious meal!

16-oz. container sour cream
13-oz. can chicken, drained
5-oz. can chicken, drained
10-3/4 oz. can cream of
   chicken soup

2 to 3 4-oz. cans diced green
   chiles
12 c. shredded Cheddar cheese,
   divided
1 doz. 6-inch corn tortillas

In a large bowl, combine all ingredients except tortillas, setting aside 3 cups cheese; mix well. Spray a 13"x9" baking pan with non-stick vegetable spray. Spread 1-1/2 cups sour cream mixture in bottom of pan. Dip each of 6 tortillas into sour cream mixture and layer in pan, overlapping slightly. Spread 5 cups sour cream mixture over top. Repeat layering with remaining tortillas and sour cream mixture; top with reserved cheese. Bake, uncovered, at 350 degrees for 25 to 35 minutes, until bubbly and golden. Let stand for 5 to 10 minutes before serving. Serves 8 to 10.

Share the cheer! Invite dinner guests to bring along
a can of food. Gather all the cans in a big wicker basket
and drop off at a local food pantry.

Slow-Cooker Shredded Chicken

Jennifer Stone
Chillicothe, OH

This recipe is a great help in my kitchen...it's a big batch of chicken that can stretch into two or more meals. The mixture of chicken breasts and thighs is moist and delicious. I like to add barbecue sauce or taco seasoning to half of the shredded chicken and leave the rest plain to add to pasta dishes.

2 lbs. frozen boneless, skinless
    chicken breasts
2 lbs. frozen boneless, skinless
    chicken thighs
salt and pepper to taste

2 c. hot water
4 cubes chicken bouillon
Optional: barbecue sauce,
    or taco seasoning mix and
    chicken broth

Layer frozen chicken pieces in a 6-quart slow cooker, sprinkling with a little salt and pepper. Pour hot water over all; tuck in bouillon cubes. Cover and cook on low setting for 8 hours, or until chicken is very tender. Remove chicken to a large bowl; cool and shred. Reserve broth in slow cooker for another recipe, if desired, or discard. May add barbecue sauce to shredded chicken, or sauté with taco seasoning and broth, or leave plain for any recipes that call for cooked chicken. Makes 16 servings, enough for 2 different recipes.

In the morning, fill up the slow cooker with a hearty dinner. After supper, you'll be able to get an early start on a cozy family evening, watching a favorite holiday movie together like *A Christmas Story* or *Miracle on 34th Street*.

Grecian Chicken Breasts

Gina McClenning
Nicholson, GA

*This is a delicious recipe that's good enough for company. It is
a tasty combination of feta cheese, spinach, garlic and
crispy bacon that will have you coming back for more.*

6 boneless, skinless chicken
    breasts
salt and pepper to taste
10-oz. pkg. frozen chopped
    spinach, thawed
8-oz. pkg. crumbled feta cheese

1/2 c. mayonnaise
1 clove garlic, minced
1/4 c. all-purpose flour
1/2 t. paprika
12 slices bacon

Cut a pocket into the side of each chicken breast. Season with salt
and pepper; set aside. Thoroughly drain and squeeze any liquid from
spinach. Add to a large bowl and mix with cheese, mayonnaise and
garlic. Stuff spinach mixture into pockets in chicken. Combine flour
and paprika in a separate bowl; lightly coat stuffed chicken breasts in
flour mixture. Wrap each chicken breast in 2 slices of bacon; place on
an ungreased rimmed baking sheet. Bake, uncovered, at 325 degrees
for one hour, or until bacon is crisp and chicken juices run clear when
pierced with a knife. Serves 6.

Try barley pilaf for a change from rice or noodles. Simply prepare
quick-cooking barley with chicken broth, seasoned with a little
chopped onion and dried parsley. Tasty, filling and speedy!

Chicken Supreme

Jeannie Heinen
McPherson, KS

My sister-in-law Mary Ann gave me this recipe, and it has become a favorite for the whole family. My grown son loves it, and my little grandson says it's his favorite too!

3 c. cooked chicken, diced
1-1/2 c. long-cooking rice, uncooked
1-1/2 c. water
1-1/2 c. shredded Cheddar cheese

2 10-3/4 oz. cans cream of chicken soup
6-oz. pkg. chicken flavored stuffing mix
1/2 c. margarine, melted
1/2 c. chicken broth

Spray a 13"x9" baking pan with non-stick vegetable spray. Add chicken, uncooked rice and water to pan; stir gently and top with cheese. Spread soup over top. In a bowl, toss together stuffing mix, margarine and broth; spread evenly on top. Bake, uncovered, at 350 degrees for 55 to 60 minutes, until hot and bubbly. Serves 8.

Baked Chicken Cutlets

Joyceann Dreibelbis
Wooster, OH

A quick & easy to prepare dish with just five ingredients. Good served with a zesty tossed salad and a steamed green vegetable.

1/2 c. Italian-flavored dry bread crumbs
3 T. grated Parmesan cheese
1/4 t. garlic powder with parsley

6 boneless, skinless chicken breasts
1/4 c. butter, melted

Combine bread crumbs, cheese and garlic powder in a shallow bowl. Dip chicken into melted butter, then into crumb mixture, coating well. Arrange chicken on a greased rimmed baking sheet. Bake at 425 degrees for 20 to 30 minutes, until golden and chicken juices run clear. Serves 6.

Boneless chicken cooks up quicker if placed in a plastic zipping bag and flattened with a meat mallet.

Rosemary Beef & Horseradish Sauce

Joshua Logan
Victoria, TX

This luscious roast beef dinner is perfect for our small family's special Christmas dinner...and it's all done in one pan! If you're not fond of parsnips, just add some more potatoes and carrots.

1 lb. fingerling potatoes
3/4 lb. parsnips, peeled and cut into chunks
1/2 lb. carrots, peeled and cut into chunks
1 T. water
3 t. olive oil, divided
4 t. fresh rosemary, chopped and divided

1 t. salt, divided
3/4 t. pepper, divided
1 lb. center-cut eye of round beef roast, 3 inches in diameter
1 t. garlic, finely chopped

In a large bowl, toss vegetables with water, 2 teaspoons oil, 3 teaspoons rosemary, 3/4 teaspoon salt and 1/2 teaspoon pepper. Rub roast with garlic and remaining olive oil, rosemary, salt and pepper. Place roast on a lightly greased rimmed baking sheet; surround with vegetables in a single layer. Bake at 450 degrees, turning vegetables once, for 20 minutes, or until a meat thermometer inserted in the center reads 145 degrees. Transfer roast to a cutting board; cover loosely with aluminum foil. Return vegetables to oven; continue baking until tender. Slice roast; serve with vegetables and Horseradish Sauce. Serves 4.

Horseradish Sauce:

1/2 c. plain Greek yogurt
2-1/2 T. prepared horseradish

2 t. white wine vinegar

Combine all ingredients; mix well. Chill until serving time.

Sing we all merrily, Christmas is here,
The day we love best of all days in the year.
–Old English poem

Slow-Simmered Italian Steak

Deirdre Edgette
Lima, OH

My sister received this slow-cooker recipe from a friend who got it from her sister! I've added a few tweaks... it's delicious and so easy.

1-1/2 lbs. stew beef cubes
1/2 c. onion, chopped
2 to 3 T. green pepper, chopped
4-oz. jar sliced mushrooms, drained
2 T. olive oil
1/3 c. chili sauce
1/4 c. green olives with pimentos, drained and sliced
1/4 c. water
1/2 t. Worcestershire sauce
1 t. salt
1/8 t. garlic salt
1/8 t. pepper

Place beef cubes in a 5-quart slow cooker; set aside. In a deep skillet over medium heat, cook onion, green pepper and mushrooms in olive oil for 5 minutes. Blend in remaining ingredients; spoon mixture over beef. Cover and cook on low setting for 6 to 8 hours, or on high setting for 4 to 4-1/2 hours. Makes 6 to 8 servings.

For a pretty yet super-speedy centerpiece, wrap chunky pillar candles in lengths of glittery wide ribbon and fasten with double-stick tape. A great way to use all those snippets of extra ribbon too!

Shrimp Victoria

Karen Pilcher
Burleson, TX

*This delicious recipe was given to me by a very good friend over
40 years ago. We still enjoy this as much now as then.*

1/2 c. butter
1-1/2 lbs. uncooked medium
   shrimp, peeled and deveined
1/2 lb. mushrooms, chopped
1/2 c. onion, finely chopped
1/4 c. green pepper, finely
   chopped

2 T. all-purpose flour
1/4 t. salt
1/8 t. cayenne pepper
8-oz. container sour cream
1/2 c. white wine or water
3 c. hot cooked rice

Melt butter in a large skillet over medium heat; add shrimp,
mushrooms, onion and green pepper. Sauté for 10 minutes, or until
vegetables are tender. Sprinkle with flour and seasonings; reduce
heat to low. Stir in sour cream and wine or water; simmer gently for
10 minutes. Do not boil. Serve shrimp and sauce with hot cooked rice.
Makes 4 to 6 servings.

Keep frozen shrimp on hand for delicious meals anytime. Let it
thaw overnight in the fridge, or to thaw quickly, place the frozen
shrimp in a colander and run ice-cold water over it.

Lemon-Rice Stuffed Cod & Broccolini

Mia Rossi
Charlotte, NC

By tradition, my Italian family always has seafood on Christmas Eve. It's often an elaborate dinner, but with this easy recipe I can serve up an all-in-one meal that everyone enjoys. Great for other busy days too.

1/4 c. onion, chopped	1 c. plain yogurt
1/4 c. celery, diced	1 lemon, peeled and halved
2 T. butter	1 lb. broccolini, trimmed
1 c. hot water	2 T. olive oil
1/8 t. salt	garlic salt and pepper to taste
1/8 t. dried thyme	6 6-oz. codfish fillets
3/4 c. long-cooking rice, uncooked	

In a large saucepan over medium heat, sauté onion and celery in butter. Add water, salt and thyme; stir in uncooked rice. Reduce heat to medium-low. Cover and simmer until rice is tender, 15 to 25 minutes. Remove from heat; stir in yogurt. Dice half of lemon and add to rice mixture; set aside. Drizzle broccolini with olive oil; add seasonings and set aside. With a thin knife, slice each fish fillet on one long edge without cutting all the way through; open up flat. Divide rice mixture evenly among fillets, placing to one side; fold other half over to close. Place stuffed fillets on a greased baking sheet. Bake, uncovered, at 350 degrees for 25 to 30 minutes, adding broccolini to pan after 10 minutes. Thinly slice remaining lemon; garnish cod and broccolini with lemon. Serves 6.

When visiting friends during the holidays, slip an ornament onto their tree with a small gift tag. When they take down the tree, it'll be a thoughtful after-Christmas surprise.

Mushroom Alfredo Pasta Bake

Krista Marshall
Fort Wayne, IN

We are pasta fanatics at our house, so I'm always looking for ways to make old recipes new again. This takes a favorite and turns it into a terrific meatless casserole, perfect for any weeknight or potluck. My son Alex immediately gave it two thumbs up!

1/2 c. plus 2 T. butter, room temperature, divided
1 lb. sliced mushrooms
3 cloves garlic, minced and divided
salt and pepper to taste
2 c. whipping cream

3/4 c. grated Parmesan cheese, divided
8-oz. pkg. shredded mozzarella cheese, divided
2 12-oz. pkgs. penne pasta, uncooked
dried parsley to taste

Melt 2 tablespoons butter in a large skillet over medium heat. Add mushrooms and one clove minced garlic; sauté until golden. Season with salt and pepper. Remove from heat; drain and set aside mixture in a bowl. Wipe out skillet; add remaining butter and melt over medium-low heat. Stir in cream and remaining garlic; bring to a simmer, stirring constantly. Add 1/2 cup Parmesan cheese and simmer for 8 to 10 minutes, stirring often, until thickened. Add 3/4 cup mozzarella cheese; stir until melted and smooth. Season with more salt and pepper; cover and remove from heat. Meanwhile, cook pasta according to package directions, just until tender; drain. To assemble, ladle enough Alfredo sauce into a greased 13"x9" baking pan to cover the bottom of pan. Layer with 1/4 each of cooked pasta, mushroom mixture, remaining Parmesan cheese, mozzarella cheese and remaining sauce. Repeat layering 3 times; sprinkle with parsley. Bake, uncovered, at 350 degrees for 15 to 20 minutes, until heated through and golden on top. Remove from oven; cover with aluminum foil. Let stand for 10 minutes before serving. Serves 6.

Make it easy on yourself when planning holiday dinners...stick to tried & true recipes! You'll find your guests are just as happy with simple comfort foods as with the most elegant gourmet meal.

Holiday Meals

Baked Salmon Fillets

Jane Martin
Havre De Grace, MD

*A quick, delicious and very elegant dinner when company's coming.
I cut the recipe in half for just two servings. I like to buy large salmon
pieces when on sale, then cut them into fillets and freeze using a
food sealer.*

1/4 c. butter, softened
2 T. lemon juice, divided
2 t. Dijon mustard

salt and pepper to taste
4 to 6 4-oz. salmon fillets

In a small bowl, mix butter, one tablespoon lemon juice and mustard
until well blended. Rub one tablespoon butter mixture over an
aluminum foil-lined baking sheet. Place fillets on pan, skin-side down.
Drizzle with remaining lemon juice; season with salt and pepper and
top with remaining butter mixture. Bake at 400 degrees for 12 to
15 minutes. Serves 4 to 6.

Golden Light Tilapia

Barbara Bargdill
Gooseberry Patch

A light & easy recipe that's less than 200 calories per serving!

1 c. corn flake cereal
2 T. all-purpose flour
1 T. seafood seasoning

4 thin tilapia fillets
1 T. butter

Crush corn flakes in a large plastic zipping bag. Add flour and
seasoning; shake to mix. Add fish fillets to bag, one at a time; close
bag and shake gently to coat with crumbs. Melt butter in a non-stick
skillet over medium heat; add fish. Cook until golden on the bottom,
about 5 minutes; turn over. Cook until fish is golden and flakes easily
with a fork, about 5 more minutes. Serves 4.

Coleslaw pairs well with fish dishes. Perk
up your favorite coleslaw with some
pineapple tidbits for a delicious change.

Nini's Sweet & Tangy Pork Tenderloin

Macey Resmondo
Lakeland, FL

When I was growing up, my Nini always made this meal for me whenever I came to visit. Once I was older, she shared the recipe with me. Every time I cook it, my house smells just like her house did when she made this. There will be plenty of sauce...it's extra yummy to dip dinner rolls or biscuits into.

3 T. butter
2 to 3-lb. pork tenderloin
salt and pepper to taste
1 c. apple jelly, apricot jam or
    1/2 c. of each

1 c. apple juice
1/2 c. Dijon mustard
2 T. cornstarch
2 T. light cream

Melt butter in a large skillet over medium heat. Add pork loin; cook until browned on all sides. Transfer pork loin to a lightly greased shallow 13"x9" baking pan. Season with salt and pepper; set aside. In same skillet, combine jelly or jam, apple juice and mustard. Cook, stirring continuously, for about 5 minutes, until blended. Spoon enough of jelly mixture over pork loin to coat nicely. Bake, uncovered, at 350 degrees for 50 minutes, basting with jelly mixture from baking pan. Remove from oven; let stand several minutes. Slice pork loin 1-1/2 inches thick; cover to keep warm. To remaining jelly mixture in skillet, add cornstarch and cream; cook and stir until thickened. Spoon sauce over sliced pork. Serves 4 to 6.

Whenever a guest asks, "How can I help?" be ready with an answer! Whether it's setting the table, filling glasses with ice or even bringing their special dessert, friends are usually happy to pitch in.

Sweet-and-Sour Spareribs

Colleen Beaudoin
Saskatchewan, Canada

*My mother's wonderful recipe...always requested for her
to make for family functions.*

2 to 4 racks side or back pork spareribs, or a combination 1 c. all-purpose flour	salt and pepper to taste 2 to 3 T. oil 1 c. onion, sliced

Cut spareribs into serving-size sections; set aside. Combine flour, salt
and pepper in a plastic zipping bag. Add ribs; seal bag and shake to
coat. Heat oil in a large skillet over medium heat; add ribs and brown
on both sides. Drain; transfer ribs to a lightly greased roasting pan and
set aside. Top with onion slices; pour Sweet-and-Sour Sauce over ribs.
Cover and bake at 325 degrees for 2 hours. Serves 4 to 6.

Sweet-and-Sour Sauce:

1 c. water	2 T. soy sauce
1/2 c. catsup	1/2 t. salt
1/2 c. brown sugar, packed	Optional: 1 T. cornstarch
1/3 c. vinegar	

Add water to the same skillet used to brown ribs; bring to a boil
over medium-high heat. Stir in remaining ingredients except
cornstarch; return to a boil. If desired, stir in cornstarch; cook and
stir until thickened.

Gather up little mittens or gloves that the children have
outgrown...they make such a sweet decoration for a front-door
wreath. Add a bow made of a child-size knitted scarf...charming!

Momma's Mexican Stew

Michelle Powell
Valley, AL

Not a soup, not a chili! This hearty stew comes together quick and tastes even better served the next day. Excellent with cornbread.

4 t. oil	14-1/2 oz. can diced tomatoes
1-1/2 lbs. stew beef cubes	16-oz. pkg. frozen corn, thawed
1 c. onion, chopped	2 c. water
1 to 2 cloves garlic, minced	1 t. salt
2 T. chili powder	1/4 t. pepper

Heat oil in a large skillet over medium heat. Add beef; brown on all sides. Add onion and garlic; cook until onion is translucent. Add chili powder; stir to coat beef. Add tomatoes with juice and remaining ingredients. Reduce heat to medium-low. Cover and simmer for one hour, or until beef is tender, stirring occasionally. Makes 6 servings.

Double Corn Muffins

Sandy Ward
Anderson, IN

So easy to make...perfect with your favorite stew or casserole.

2 8-1/2 oz. pkgs. corn muffin mix	2 eggs, beaten
14-3/4 oz. can creamed corn	8-oz. container sour cream
	1/2 c. onion, chopped

Combine all ingredients in a large bowl. Stir just until moistened but still slightly lumpy. Pour batter into greased muffin cups, filling 2/3 full. Bake at 350 degrees for 25 to 35 minutes, until a toothpick test clean. Makes 1-1/2 to 2 dozen.

Wide-rimmed soup plates are perfect for serving saucy pasta dishes as well as hearty dinner portions of stew. There's even room to balance a muffin or roll on the edge.

Crazy Crust Sausage Pizza

Patricia Nau
River Grove, IL

This recipe is so easy and so delicious. Perfect for those busy days we all have in December! Very easy to make just the way your family likes it too.

2 16-oz. pkgs. mild and/or hot
   Italian pork sausage
1 c. all-purpose flour
2 eggs, beaten
2/3 c. milk
1 t. kosher salt
1 t. dried oregano

Optional: chopped onions,
   tomatoes, green pepper,
   mushrooms, olives
2 15-oz. cans pizza sauce
8-oz. pkg. shredded mozzarella
   cheese, or more to taste

In a large skillet over medium heat, brown sausage. Drain; remove from heat and let stand for 15 to 20 minutes. Meanwhile, in a bowl, mix together flour, eggs, milk and seasonings. Pour batter into a greased rimmed baking sheet, tilting to cover edges. Spread sausage on batter to cover pan; add other toppings as desired. Bake at 425 degrees for 25 minutes; remove from oven. Spread pizza sauce on top; cover completely with cheese. Return to oven and bake another 10 minutes, or until bubbly and cheese is melted. Serves 4 to 6.

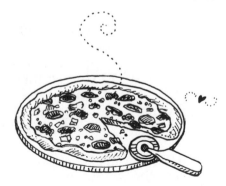

Looking for fun ideas for the holiday week when the kids are home from school? Host a daytime pajama party for younger kids who want to try a sleepover, but aren't quite ready to sleep away from home. Invite guests to arrive in late afternoon, already dressed in PJ's. They can enjoy movies, pizza and all the fun of a slumber party, then go home by early evening to their own beds.

Chicken & Biscuit Casserole

Paige Miller
Mansfield, OH

This is a wonderful warm, cozy meal for a chilly night.

2 boneless, skinless chicken
   breasts, diced
1/4 c. onion
1 T. butter
10-3/4 oz. can cream of chicken
   soup

8-oz. container sour cream
1/2 c. whole milk
8-oz. pkg. shredded mild
   Cheddar cheese
7-1/2 oz. tube refrigerated
   biscuits

In a skillet over medium heat, sauté chicken and onion in butter until chicken is cooked through and onion is translucent. Stir in soup, sour cream and milk; transfer mixture to a greased 13"x9" baking pan. Bake, uncovered, at 350 degrees for 30 minutes. Remove from oven; spread cheese evenly on top. Arrange biscuits over cheese. Return to oven. Bake another 14 to 15 minutes, until biscuits are golden and cheese is melted. Serves 6.

Turkey Pot Pie

Susan Lane
La Grange, NC

Handed down through three generations...very easy
and good tasting.

2 9-inch pie crusts
1 c. evaporated milk
0.87-oz. pkg. turkey gravy mix
1/2 t. dried thyme

2 c. roast turkey, shredded
10-oz. pkg. frozen mixed
   vegetables, thawed
1 c. shredded Cheddar cheese

Arrange one pie crust in a 9" pie plate; set aside. In a bowl, combine remaining ingredients except cheese. Mix well and spoon into crust. Break up remaining crust on top of pie; top with cheese. Bake at 400 degrees for 40 minutes, or until bubbly and golden. Serves 8.

For a beautiful golden pie crust, beat an egg yolk and brush it thinly over the crust before you pop it in the oven.

Family Scalloped Potatoes & Ham

Sandra Clay
Potterville, MI

This old-fashioned recipe has been passed down through my family until it has become part of our traditions. It shows up at many of our family gatherings.

10-3/4 oz. can can cream of
    mushroom soup
2 c. milk
salt and pepper to taste
5 lbs. Yukon Gold potatoes,
    peeled, cubed or sliced
    and divided

3/4 c. onion, diced and divided
3 c. shredded sharp Cheddar
    cheese, divided
2 c. smoked ham, cubed or
    sliced and divided

In a bowl, whisk together soup and milk; season with salt and pepper. In a greased deep 3-quart casserole dish, layer half each of potatoes, onion, cheese, ham and soup mixture; repeat layering. Cover with aluminum foil. Bake at 375 degrees for 1-1/2 hours, or until heated through and potatoes are tender. Serves 8 to 10.

Fill vintage Mason jars with small, shiny vintage ornament balls. Group several jars for a splendid centerpiece...a great way to use those ornaments that have lost their hangers.

Chicken & Orzo Dinner

Eileen Steitz-Watts
Cape Coral, FL

With the help of a rotisserie chicken, this recipe is easy
to make. We love the combination of flavors.

8-oz. pkg. orzo pasta,
  uncooked
1 deli rotisserie chicken,
  shredded, bones and skin
  discarded
3 c. fresh baby spinach

1 c. crumbled blue cheese or
  less, according to taste
2 c. grape tomatoes, cut in half
1/2 c. pitted Kalamata olives
2 T. olive oil
salt and pepper to taste

Cook pasta according to directions on package; drain. Return pasta to
cooking pot; stir in remaining ingredients. Cook over medium heat
until heated through, about 3 minutes. Makes 4 to 6 servings.

Invite friends to join you for a favorite weeknight skillet
or slow-cooker meal in December...a meal shared with
friends doesn't need to be fancy. After all, it's friendship
that makes it special!

Pork Tenderloin Diane

Sue Klapper
Muskego, WI

I love to serve this elegant main dish to special guests. They never suspect that it is healthy as well as delicious!

1-lb. pork tenderloin, sliced into 8 pieces	2 T. lemon juice
2 t. lemon pepper	1 T. Worcestershire sauce
2 T. butter	1 t. Dijon mustard
	1 T. fresh chives, finely chopped

Flatten each tenderloin piece into a medallion, one inch thick. Season with lemon pepper; set aside. Melt butter in a large heavy skillet over medium heat. Add pork; cook for 3 to 4 minutes on each side. Remove pork to a serving platter; cover to keep warm. Add lemon juice, Worcestershire sauce and mustard to pan juices in the skillet. Cook and stir until heated through. Spoon the sauce over pork medallions; sprinkle with chives. Serves 4.

Just for fun, set the kids down after Christmas with cast-off wrapping paper and a paper punch. You'll have a bowlful of confetti for New Year's Eve in no time at all!

Lasagna Roll-Ups

Sue Bogumil
West Seneca, NY

I first made this recipe for a Christmas party with some of my closest friends. It was a great evening, and I've made it many times since. It's also wonderful to make ahead of time to deliver, unbaked, to a friend. Send along the baking instructions and a loaf of crusty bread to make someone's day extra special!

8 slices center-cut bacon, diced
1 c. onion, diced
1 clove garlic, minced
salt and pepper to taste
2 28-oz. cans crushed tomatoes
1 lb. ground beef
1/8 t. red pepper flakes

24 lasagna noodles, uncooked
5 c. ricotta cheese
1 c. grated Parmesan cheese
4 eggs, lightly beaten
1 t. onion powder
8-oz. pkg. shredded mozzarella
   cheese

In a Dutch oven over medium heat, cook bacon until almost crisp; do not drain. Add onion; cook until translucent. Sprinkle with garlic, salt and pepper. Cook for one to 2 minutes, being careful not to burn. Stir in tomatoes with juice; bring to a boil. Reduce heat to low. Cover and simmer for one hour, stirring occasionally. Meanwhile, brown beef in a skillet over medium heat; drain. Add beef and red pepper flakes to sauce; continue simmering for another hour. Cook lasagna noodles according to package directions; drain. To assemble, spread half of sauce in a greased 13"x9" baking pan; set aside. In a bowl, blend ricotta and Parmesan cheeses, eggs and onion powder. Spread 1/4 cup of cheese mixture onto each noodle; roll up and place seam-side down over sauce in pan. Top roll-ups with remaining sauce and mozzarella cheese. Cover and bake at 375 degrees for 30 to 35 minutes, until heated through and cheese is melted. Let stand 10 minutes before serving. Serves 8 to 12.

Make a trivet to protect the tabletop from hot dishes. Simply glue a cork square to the bottom of a large ceramic tile.

Sweets
OF THE SEASON

Forgotten Cookies

Cindy Williams
Owensboro, KY

These cookies are very airy and light...they will melt in your mouth.
They are very easy to make too. I received this unique recipe many
years ago from a close friend who was like family to me. She made
them every Christmas for her family. She has since passed away, so
these hold special memories for me. I have made them myself for
many years now.

3 egg whites, room temperature
1/8 t. salt
2/3 c. sugar
1/2 t. vanilla extract

6-oz. pkg. semi-sweet chocolate
  chips
1 c. chopped pecans
Optional: 24 pecan halves

Preheat oven to 350 degrees. In a deep bowl with an electric mixer on
high speed, beat egg whites until soft peaks form. Add salt; gradually
beat in sugar. Continue beating until stiff peaks form; add vanilla.
Use a spoon to fold in chocolate chips and pecans; set aside. Spray
2 aluminum foil-lined baking sheets with non-stick vegetable spray.
Drop mixture by teaspoonfuls onto baking sheets. If desired, top each
cookie with a pecan half. Place in preheated oven; immediately turn
oven off. Leave cookies in oven for 2 hours to overnight. Gently
remove from baking sheet with a spatula; store in an airtight container.
Makes 2 dozen.

Cheery holiday potholders with pockets can be found at
any grocery. Slip several wrapped cookies (and the recipe!)
into the pocket for handy gifts.

Sweets
OF THE SEASON

Dutch Butter Cookies

Becky Kuchenbecker
Ravenna, OH

When I was in high school, one of my teachers brought these cookies into class. I asked if she would share this recipe with me...I've been making them ever since! I always top off my cookie trays with these cookies, decorated with red & green sprinkles for Christmas, red for Valentine's Day and so forth.

1 c. butter
1 c. sugar
1 egg, beaten
2-1/2 c. all-purpose flour
1 t. baking powder

2 t. vanilla extract
1/4 t. salt
Garnish: colored sprinkles or
    colored sugar

In a large bowl, blend together butter and sugar. Add egg; mix well. Add remaining ingredients except garnish; mix again. Spread dough thinly in a greased 15"x10" jelly-roll pan. Drag a fork across dough to draw lines. Sprinkle with colored sprinkles or sugar. Bake at 325 degrees for 20 to 25 minutes, until lightly golden. While still warm, cut into strips about 2 inches wide, then into bars 1-1/2 inches wide. Cool cookies in pan for 5 minutes; remove cookies to a wire rack and cool completely. Makes 3 to 4 dozen.

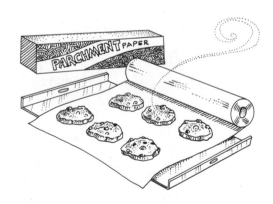

Parchment paper is a baker's best friend. Place it on a baking sheet to keep cookies from spreading and sticking. Clean-up is a breeze too...just toss away the paper.

No-Bake Coconut Macaroon Kisses

Joyce Sipe
New Wilmington, PA

We often made these cookies at Christmas time. They're a quick and tasty cookie treat we'd make whenever someone else was using the oven. All of my family loved coconut, so these went over quite well. I remember my mother and me singing Christmas carols (with the music turned up loud to drown out our terrible voices!) while we worked in the kitchen making cookies for the family get-together.

7-oz. pkg. flaked coconut
2 c. powdered sugar
1/2 c. powdered milk
1/4 c. candied red cherries,
    chopped
1/4 c. candied green cherries,
    chopped

3 T. water
2 t. butter, melted
1 t. almond extract
24 milk chocolate drops,
    unwrapped

In a large bowl, combine all ingredients except chocolate drops; mix well. Drop coconut mixture by rounded tablespoonfuls onto wax paper-lined baking sheets. Press a chocolate drop into the top of each mound. Refrigerate for 30 minutes, or until firm. Makes 2 dozen.

Create a sweet goodie bag from a plain paper sack! Fold the top over, punch 2 holes and slide a peppermint stick through.

Sweets
OF THE SEASON

Best-Ever Shortbread Cookies *Charlene Riddell*
Ontario, Canada

This is a recipe handed down from my mother-in-law. They are the best melt-in-your-mouth shortbread and the easiest to make... a must every year for our Christmas cookie tray. You can add any embellishments you like. Colored sugar and candied red and green cherries cut up and arranged like a poinsettia flower are just a couple I like to use.

1 c. butter	3 c. all-purpose flour
1 c. margarine	1/2 t. salt
1/2 c. cornstarch	Optional: colored sugar, candied
1 c. powdered sugar	red and green cherries

In a large bowl, blend together butter and margarine. Stir in cornstarch; beat together. Gradually add powdered sugar, beating until creamy. Gradually beat in flour and salt until light and fluffy. Drop dough by teaspoonfuls onto ungreased baking sheets. If baking on more than one sheet, beat the batter again each time before adding more cookies to the baking sheet to ensure a melt-in-your mouth texture. Decorate cookies with colored sugar or candied cherries, if desired. Bake at 350 degrees for 8 to 10 minutes, just until dough lightly golden. Cool on wire racks. Makes 5 dozen.

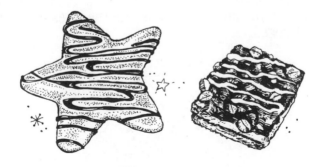

Dress up cookies with a drizzle of chocolate in a jiffy!
Fill a plastic zipping bag with chocolate chips and
microwave briefly, until melted. Snip off a tiny corner
and drizzle away...afterwards, just toss away the bag.

Gingerbread Men

Cassie Hooker
La Porte, TX

This recipe has been used by our family for over 50 years now. When I was a little girl, I would bake these cookies with my mother. We would decorate them, then wrap them individually in plastic wrap, tie with a ribbon and hang them on the Christmas tree. I also did this with my two daughters when they were little. The gingerbread men always looked sweet hanging on our tree, along with the strings of popcorn we put on our tree every year.

1 c. shortening
1 c. sugar
1/2 t. salt
1 egg, beaten
1 c. molasses
2 T. vinegar
5 c. all-purpose flour, sifted

1-1/2 t. baking soda
1 T. ground ginger
1 t. ground cloves
1 t. cinnamon
Garnish: frosting, red cinnamon
　　candies

In a large bowl, beat together shortening, sugar and salt very well. Stir in egg, molasses and vinegar; beat well and set aside. In a separate bowl, combine flour, baking soda and spices; mix well and stir into shortening mixture. Cover and chill for 2 to 3 hours. On a lightly floured surface, roll out dough 1/8-inch thick. Cut with a gingerbread man cookie cutter. Place cookies on greased baking sheets, one inch apart. Bake at 375 degrees for about 6 minutes. Cool cookies on a wire rack; decorate with frosting and candies for the faces and buttons. Makes about 4 dozen.

A great basic cookie frosting recipe...one cup powdered sugar and 2 to 3 tablespoons milk, added a little time to a spreading consistency. Stir in one teaspoon vanilla or almond extract and tint with a drop or 2 of food coloring.

Sweets

OF THE SEASON

Beth's Toffee Bars

Beth Richter
Canby, MN

I first made these when I needed a simple recipe for a potluck. They are so good! Now if I don't bring them to family functions, I am in big trouble! Officially, the recipe serves 24 to 36, but if I don't cut them ahead of time, the number of servings has been known to be reduced to four to six. First come, first served!

18-1/2 oz. pkg. yellow cake mix
1 egg, beaten
1/3 c. butter, melted

8-oz. pkg. toffee baking bits
14-oz. can sweetened
   condensed milk

Combine dry cake mix, egg and butter in a large bowl; mix together with your hands. Gently pat mixture into a greased 13"x9" baking pan. Sprinkle toffee pieces over the top; pour condensed milk over the top. Bake at 350 degrees for about 25 minutes. Cool in pan on a wire rack. Cut into bars. Makes 2 to 3 dozen.

Nut & Candy Cookie Bars

Marlene Burns
Swisher, IA

Such a fun recipe! Use red and green candies for Christmastime.

18-1/4 oz. pkg. dark chocolate
   fudge cake mix
2 eggs, beaten
1/2 c. butter, melted
14-oz. can sweetened condensed
   milk
1/2 c. sweetened flaked coconut

1/2 c. lightly salted roasted
   mixed nuts
1/2 c. mini semi-sweet chocolate
   chips
1/2 c. mini candy-coated
   chocolates

Combine dry cake mix, eggs and butter in a large bowl; beat until smooth and blended. Press into an aluminum foil-lined 13"x9" baking pan. Bake at 325 degrees for 25 minutes. Pour condensed milk over warm crust in pan. Sprinkle with remaining ingredients. Return to oven for another 15 minutes, or until set. Cool in pan on a wire rack. Cut into bars. Makes 1-1/2 dozen.

Gingerbread Squares

Donna Wilson
Maryville, TN

*I just love gingerbread! So this is one way we enjoy it at our house.
When it's in the oven, it makes the house smell so yummy.*

1/2 c. butter, softened	1-1/2 c. all-purpose flour
1/2 c. brown sugar, packed	1 t. baking soda
1/2 c. boiling water	1 t. cinnamon
1/2 c. dark molasses	1 t. ground ginger
1 egg, beaten	1/4 t. ground cloves

In a large bowl, combine butter, brown sugar, boiling water, molasses
and egg; mix well. Add remaining ingredients; mix again. Pour batter
into a greased 8"x8" baking pan. Bake at 350 degrees for 30 minutes,
or until a toothpick tests clean. Cut into squares. Makes 9 servings.

Margaret's Christmas Candy

Becca Jones
Jackson, TN

*Every year, my friend makes at least a dozen different kinds of
Christmas goodies. This is one of the favorites.*

2-1/4 lbs. white melting chocolate	2 c. salted peanuts
	3 c. crispy rice cereal
Optional: 1 drop red food coloring	1 c. creamy peanut butter
	2 c. mini marshmallows

Melt chocolate in the top of a large double boiler over hot water,
stirring constantly. If desired, stir in food coloring. Add remaining
ingredients; stir until well blended. Drop mixture by tablespoonfuls
onto wax paper; cool until set. Makes 12 to 15 servings.

A quick-as-a-wink table runner...
lay wide ribbon across the
table's length and width.

Sweets
OF THE SEASON

Big Bowl of Chocolate

Martha Stapler
Sanford, FL

When I first began making this brownie trifle for luncheons at work, I did not have a name for it, so my friend named it "The Big Bowl of Chocolate." Scrumptious!

18-oz. pkg. brownie mix
3.9-oz. pkg. instant chocolate
   pudding mix
2 c. milk
16-oz. container frozen whipped
   topping, thawed and divided

21-oz. can cherry pie filling,
   divided
Garnish: chocolate candy bars,
   broken in pieces

Prepare and bake brownies according to package instructions. Cool completely; crumble brownies and set aside. Meanwhile, combine pudding mix and milk in a bowl. Beat with an electric mixer on low speed for 2 minutes, or until thickened. Cover and chill. To assemble, layer in a glass trifle bowl as follows: 1/2 of brownies, 1/2 of pudding, 1/3 of whipped topping and 1/2 of pie filling. Repeat layering; spread remaining topping over all. Garnish with candy bar pieces. Cover and refrigerate overnight before serving. Makes 10 to 15 servings.

Make time for your town's special holiday events. Whether it's a Christmas parade, Santa arriving by horse-drawn sleigh or a tree lighting ceremony, hometown traditions make the best memories!

Crazy-Good Cranberry Crunch

Marsha Baker
Pioneer, OH

*This dish always satisfies my craving for cranberry sauce. I love
the crunch of the nuts and oats along with the brown sugar.
It's a favorite holiday dessert.*

1 c. old-fashioned or
   quick-cooking oats,
   uncooked
1/2 c. all-purpose flour
3/4 c. brown sugar, packed
6 T. butter, softened

14-oz. can whole-berry
   cranberry sauce
Optional: 1/2 c. chopped nuts,
   1/4 t. freshly grated nutmeg
Garnish: ice cream or whipped
   topping

In a large bowl, combine oats, flour and brown sugar; cut in butter with
a fork or pastry blender until crumbly. Press half of crumb mixture into
the bottom of a greased 9" pie plate or 8"x8" baking pan to form a
crust; set aside. Spoon cranberry sauce into a bowl; stir until spreadable.
Dollop cranberry sauce over crust; spread evenly over crust with the
back of the spoon. Top with remaining crumb mixture; sprinkle with
nuts and nutmeg, if desired. Bake at 350 degrees for 45 minutes,
or until bubbly and golden. Serve warm, topped with ice cream or
whipped topping. Serves 6.

If brown sugar has hardened in its bag, tuck a moistened paper
towel into the bag and microwave it for 20 seconds. Repeat for
another 10 seconds if needed. Soft and ready to use!

Pecan-Oatmeal Cheesecake Pie

Julie Pak
Henryetta, OK

This pie is like having three old-fashioned pie recipes rolled into one! It's a favorite at our house at Christmastime.

8-oz. cream cheese, room
   temperature
4 eggs, divided
3/4 c. sugar, divided
2 t. vanilla extract, divided
1/2 t. salt, divided

9-inch pie crust, unbaked
1 c. old-fashioned oats,
   uncooked
1/2 c. chopped pecans
1 c. light corn syrup
1/2 t. cinnamon

In a large bowl, combine cream cheese, one egg, 1/2 cup sugar, one teaspoon vanilla and 1/4 teaspoon salt. With an electric mixer on medium speed, beat together until smooth. Pour into unbaked pie crust. In a separate bowl, stir together oats and pecans; spread evenly over cream cheese mixture. In another bowl, whisk together corn syrup, cinnamon and remaining eggs, sugar, vanilla and salt. Pour mixture evenly over oat mixture. Set pie plate on a baking sheet; place on lowest oven rack. Bake at 425 degrees for 15 minutes. Reduce oven to 350 degrees; continue baking another 30 to 35 minutes, until set. Cool completely on a wire rack. Once cooled, may cover and refrigerate up to 2 days. Makes 8 servings.

A tiered serving stand is just right for holding a variety
of cookies and candies for get-togethers.

Butterscotch Holiday Cookies

Kay Kingsley
Indianapolis, IN

Best-ever in the sugar cookie category! These are the cookies that we would set out for Santa back in the 1940s when I was a little girl. Must be the brown sugar and lemon juice that make them so special.

3/4 c. butter
1 c. light brown sugar, packed
1 egg, well beaten
1/2 t. lemon juice
1 t. vanilla extract

2-1/2 c. all-purpose flour
1 t. baking powder
1/8 t. baking soda
1/4 t. salt
Garnish: colored sugars

In a large bowl, blend butter, brown sugar, egg, lemon juice and vanilla; set aside. Into a separate bowl, sift flour. Measure and sift again, adding baking powder, baking soda and salt. Add flour mixture gradually to butter mixture, beating well after each addition. Cover and chill until firm enough to roll. Roll out dough 1/8-inch thick on a lightly floured surface. Cut with cookie cutters; arrange on ungreased baking sheets. Garnish with colored sugars. Bake at 450 degrees for about 6 minutes, until golden; watch closely to avoid browning on the bottom. Cool on a wire rack. Makes about 6 dozen.

Sprinkle powdered sugar on the work surface when rolling out sugar cookie dough...so much tastier than using flour and it works just as well!

Sweets
OF THE SEASON

Candy Cane Peppermint Kiss Cookies

Suzanne Ramey
Allendale, MI

If you like peppermint, you will love these cookies! They have crushed peppermint candies in the dough and a candy cane chocolate kiss on the top. They are rolled in sugar to give them a pretty sparkle. Perfect for Christmas cookie trays or for gift giving.

1 c. butter, softened
1 t. peppermint extract
10 peppermint candies, very
    finely crushed
2 c. all-purpose flour

1 c. sugar, divided
1/4 t. salt
10-oz. pkg. candy cane
    white chocolate drops

In a large bowl, blend together butter and extract; beat in crushed candies. Add flour, 1/2 cup sugar and salt; stir well. Cover and chill for 30 to 60 minutes. Roll dough into one-inch balls; roll in remaining sugar. Place on lightly greased baking sheets. Bake at 350 degrees for about 12 minutes. Immediately press a chocolate drop in the center of each cookie. Cool cookies on baking sheets for several minutes; remove to a wire rack and cool completely. Makes 3 dozen.

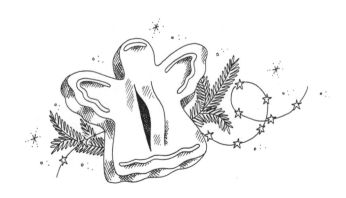

It is Christmas in the heart that puts
Christmas in the air.

–W.T. Ellis

Swedish Orange Ginger Cookies

Karen Crooks
West Des Moines, IA

This recipe was given to my grandmother more than 50 years ago by her best friend Ida. It can be rolled out for cut-out cookies or formed into refrigerator rolls for slice & bake convenience. The touch of orange zest with the ginger is wonderful!

1 c. butter, softened
1-1/2 c. sugar
1 egg, beaten
1-1/2 T. orange zest
2 T. dark corn syrup
1 T. water

3-1/4 c. all-purpose flour
2 t. baking soda
2 t. cinnamon
1 t. ground ginger
1/2 t. ground cloves

In a large bowl, blend together butter and sugar. Add egg; beat until light and fluffy. Add orange zest, corn syrup and water; mix well and set aside. In a separate bowl, sift together remaining ingredients; stir into butter mixture. Cover and chill thoroughly. On a lightly floured surface, roll out dough 1/8-inch thick; cut with cookie cutters. Dough may also be rolled into logs; refrigerate or freeze until ready to slice and bake, then slice 1/4-inch to 3/8-inch thick. For either style of cookie, place on parchment paper-lined baking sheets. Bake at 350 degrees for 8 to 10 minutes, depending on whether you want your cookies soft or crisp. Makes 2 to 3 dozen.

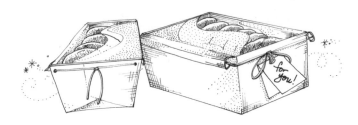

Mailing cookies to a friend? Select sturdy cookies that won't crumble easily. Bar cookies, brownies and drop cookies travel well, while frosted or filled cookies may be too soft. Pack cookies in single layers in a sturdy box, with wax paper between the layers. Your cookies will arrive fresh, unbroken and full of love!

French Christmas Cookies

Tamela James
Grove City, OH

I first tried this recipe ten years ago, and it quickly become one of my husband's favorite cookies. I tucked them in the freezer for the Christmas trays. The first time he saw me putting the cookies out on the trays, he thought I had been hiding them from him! I had to explain that I had made them for him too.

1/2 c. butter, softened	2 c. pecans, finely chopped
1 c. brown sugar, packed	2-3/4 c. milk chocolate chips,
1 c. milk	divided
2-3/4 c. graham cracker crumbs	

In a large bowl, beat butter and brown sugar until light and fluffy. Beat in milk; stir in cracker crumbs, pecans and 2 cups chocolate chips. Spoon batter into mini foil baking cups, filling 3/4 full. Set cups on baking sheets, 2 inches apart. Bake at 375 degrees for 10 to 12 minutes, until set. Cool on wire racks. Melt remaining chocolate; spoon a small amount of chocolate onto each cookie. Keep refrigerated. Makes about 9 dozen.

Almond Snowballs

Lisa Langston
Conroe, TX

I have had this recipe more than 35 years. It's a Christmas cookie I make every year.

1/2 c. butter, softened	1/4 c. sugar
1-1/2 t. vanilla extract	1/8 t. salt
1 c. all-purpose flour	Garnish: powdered sugar
1-1/2 c. almonds, finely ground	

In a large bowl, blend together butter and vanilla. Mix in flour, almonds, sugar and salt until dough comes together. Roll dough into balls by tablespoonfuls; place on parchment paper-lined baking sheets. Bake at 300 degrees for 30 minutes. Remove from oven; roll cookies in powdered sugar until coated. Cool; store in a covered container. Makes about 1-1/2 dozen.

Mrs. Claus's Microwave Fudge

Mary Willet
Lincoln, NE

Every December for over 30 years, my husband and I have played Santa & Mrs. Claus and do house calls. We so enjoy the faces of the kids...even the bigger kids! We paid a visit to one seven-year-old girl who was in awe of Mrs. Claus. She asked so many questions about baking for the elves. The following year I brought her my fudge recipe to make with her grandma. She was so excited! I like to make one batch with nuts and one without nuts to share with neighbors.

32-oz. pkg. powdered sugar
1 c. baking cocoa
1/2 t. salt
1 c. butter, sliced

1/2 c. fat-free half-and-half
1/8 t. vanilla extract
Optional: 1 to 1-1/2 c. chopped
  nuts

Mix powdered sugar, cocoa and salt in a large microwave-safe bowl. Add butter and half-and-half on top. Microwave on high for 3 to 5 minutes, until butter is melted. Add vanilla; stir until smooth. Add nuts, if desired. Pour fudge into a 13"x9" baking pan lined with wax paper or parchment paper. Let set in refrigerator; cut into squares. Makes 3 dozen.

Fudge cut-outs are oh-so-simple to make and really dress up a dessert tray. Pour hot fudge into a jelly-roll pan and chill until set. Use mini cookie cutters to cut out stars, trees and other holiday shapes, then press on candy sprinkles. So sweet!

Peanut Butter Balls

Deanna Martinez-Bey
Wake Forest, NC

This recipe came from my Great-Aunt Mary, and it's very special to me. Every year she would make these at Christmastime and add them to her Christmas cookie platter. I remember digging under all of the other cookies just to find a peanut butter ball!

2 c. chunky peanut butter
1/2 c. butter, room temperature
2 c. powdered sugar
2 c. crispy rice cereal
1 c. milk chocolate chips

8-oz. pkg. semi-sweet baking
  chocolate, chopped
2 T. paraffin baking wax,
  chopped

In a large bowl, combine peanut butter, butter, powdered sugar and cereal. Mix well, using your hands; form into one-inch balls. If mixture is too sticky to shape, chill for 30 minutes before rolling. Place balls onto wax paper-lined baking sheets; refrigerate while preparing the coating. Combine remaining ingredients in a double boiler. Cook over hot water until melted; stir until smooth. Using a toothpick or fork, dip balls into chocolate. Return to baking sheets and refrigerate. Keep refrigerated in an airtight container. Makes 2 to 3 dozen.

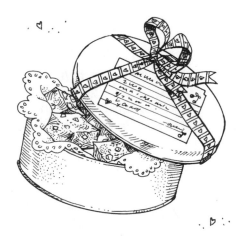

Dig into Grandma's recipe box for that extra-special treat you remember...and then bake it to share with the whole family! Don't forget to share copies of the recipe. Sure to be appreciated!

Quick & Easy Peanut Clusters

Hailey Coss
Winter, WI

When I made this recipe for the county fair 4-H judging, I won Best of Show! It's now a favorite Christmas candy that we make.

12-oz. pkg. semi-sweet
  chocolate chips
12-oz. pkg. butterscotch chips

12-oz. jar dry-roasted peanuts
1 c. toffee baking bits

Combine chocolate chips and butterscotch chips in the top of a double boiler. Stir frequently over low to medium heat until melted; add peanuts and stir. Let cool slightly; add toffee pieces and stir. Drop mixture by teaspoonfuls onto wax paper. Allow to set at room temperature. Makes 3 dozen.

Oh-So-Easy Peanut Butter Fudge

Cindy Neel
Gooseberry Patch

This fudge is beyond easy! It has even more flavor after a couple of days. Great for gifts!

2 c. sugar
1/2 c. milk

1 t. vanilla extract
3/4 c. creamy peanut butter

In a heavy saucepan over medium-high heat, bring sugar and milk to a boil. Boil for 2-1/2 minutes; remove from heat. Stir in vanilla and peanut butter. Immediately pour into a buttered 8"x8" baking pan. Allow to set; cut into squares. Store in an airtight container. Makes 2 dozen.

A recipe for success...always make candy just one batch at a time. Don't be tempted to double or triple the recipe, because the candy may fail to set up properly.

White Chocolate Pretzel Brittle

Vickie
Gooseberry Patch

A chocolatey, crunchy treat that's a snap to make. If you're a big fan of sweet & salty flavors, give it a sprinkle of coarse salt...add some red & green sugar just for fun!

4 c. bite-size crispy rice cereal squares
2 c. pretzel sticks, coarsely broken
1 c. cashews or peanuts, coarsely chopped
8-oz. pkg. white chocolate candy coating, chopped
1/2 c. semi-sweet chocolate chips

In a large bowl, combine cereal, pretzels and nuts; toss to mix and set aside. Place candy coating in a large microwave-safe bowl. Microwave on high for 1-1/2 to 2-1/2 minutes, stirring every 30 seconds, until melted and smooth. Pour over cereal mixture; stir until well coated. Press mixture into a greased 13"x9" baking pan; set aside to cool slightly. In a small microwave-safe bowl, microwave chocolate chips on high for one minute; stir until smooth. Drizzle chocolate over cereal mixture. Let stand until chocolate is set; break into clusters. Store in an airtight container. Makes about 2 dozen.

Need a gift for a special family? Give a board game or a couple of card games along with a tin filled with homemade goodies. It'll be much appreciated on the next snow day!

Peppermint Freeze

Betty Lou Wright
Hendersonville, TN

I found this recipe in the newspaper 40 years ago, and it remains a Christmas favorite. It's well worth the time it takes to prepare. My grown son insists that it be made in the same old beat-up aluminum pan that I've used since he was a little boy. Mmm...it's wintertime in a pan!

2 c. vanilla wafers, crushed
1/4 c. butter, melted
1/2 c. butter, softened
2 c. powdered sugar
2 1-oz. sqs. unsweetened baking chocolate, melted and cooled

1 t. vanilla extract
3 pasteurized eggs, separated
1 qt. peppermint ice cream, softened
1 c. chopped pecans

In a bowl, combine wafer crumbs and melted butter. Press firmly and evenly into an ungreased 13"x9" baking pan; set aside. In a separate bowl, blend softened butter and powdered sugar until light and fluffy. Add chocolate, vanilla and egg yolks; beat well and set aside. In a deep bowl, beat egg whites with an electric mixer on high speed until stiff peaks form. Fold egg whites into chocolate mixture. Spread mixture evenly over crumb crust. Cover and chill for 4 hours, or until firm. Spread softened ice cream over chocolate mixture. Sprinkle with chopped pecans, lightly pressing nuts into ice cream. Cover and freeze for 3 to 4 hours. Serves 10 to 12.

Stir up some memories...invite Grandma & Grandpa to read Christmas stories to little ones and share holiday stories from their childhood.

Sweets

OF THE SEASON

Christmas Snow Pie

Judy Lange
Imperial, PA

A snow-topped holiday favorite. This recipe makes two pies...
just right for lots of company, or surprise a friend with a pie!

14-oz. can sweetened
   condensed milk
1/3 c. lemon juice
1/2 t. pineapple extract
1/3 c. sweetened flaked coconut
1/2 c. chopped pecans

15-1/4 oz. can crushed
   pineapple, drained
12-oz. container frozen whipped
   topping, thawed
2 8-inch pie crusts, baked

In a large bowl, combine all ingredients except whipped topping and
pie crusts. Mix well; fold in whipped topping. Spoon into cooled pie
crusts. Cover and chill for one hour to overnight. Makes 2 pies; each
serves 6.

Graham Cracker
Peppermint Bark

Tina Butler
Royse City, TX

Peppermint and chocolate go perfectly together! This is one of
my favorite easy-peasy Christmas cookie tray treats.

12-oz. pkg. milk chocolate
   melting chocolate
8 to 10 whole graham crackers,
   each broken into 4 pieces

2 candy canes, crushed
Optional: mini milk chocolate
   chips

Place chocolate in a microwave-safe bowl. Microwave on defrost for
6 minutes, or until melted; stir until smooth. With a fork, dip each
graham cracker into chocolate to coat; let excess drip off. Place on a
parchment-lined baking sheet. Sprinkle with crushed candy and mini
chocolate chips, if desired. Allow to set about 30 minutes. Break into
pieces or leave whole. Store in an airtight container in a cool, dry place
up to one week. Makes about 3-1/2 dozen.

Paper cupcake liners come in all colors...great for serving
single portions of fudge and other treats.

Pumpkin Spice Gingerbread

Joy Tiggemann
Minneapolis, MN

When my kids were little, we would make this in two pans.
One child added raisins to hers and the other added chocolate chips
to his. Icing is optional...a sprinkle of powered sugar is nice too.

3 c. sugar
1 c. oil
4 eggs, beaten
2/3 c. water
15-oz. can pumpkin
2 t. ground ginger
1 t. ground cloves
1 t. allspice

1 t. cinnamon
3-1/2 c. all-purpose flour
1/2 t. baking powder
2 t. baking soda
1-1/2 t. salt
Garnish: 16-oz. container cream
  cheese icing, or powdered
  sugar

In a large bowl, combine sugar, oil and eggs; beat with an electric mixer
on medium speed until smooth. Add water; beat until well blended.
Stir in pumpkin and spices; set aside. In a separate bowl, combine
remaining ingredients except garnish. Add flour mixture to pumpkin
mixture; blend just until well mixed. Spread batter in a lightly greased
15"x10" jelly-roll pan. Bake at 350 degrees for 35 to 40 minutes, until
a toothpick tests clean. Cool completely. Spread with frosting or
sprinkle with powdered sugar. Serves 20.

Happy holiday, happy holiday,
While the merry bells keep ringing
May your every wish come true.

–Irving Berlin

Sweets

OF THE SEASON

Easy Apple Kuchen

Melanie Springer
Canton, OH

*I made this for my husband the first year we were married.
Now, 45 years later, it is still a true family favorite. I still have
to bake at least one every year for Christmas for my family!*

18-1/2 oz. pkg. yellow cake mix
1/2 c. butter, softened
1/2 c. sweetened flaked coconut
20-oz. can sliced apples,
    drained, or 2 baking apples,
    peeled, cored and sliced

1/2 c. sugar
1 t. cinnamon
1 egg, lightly beaten
8-oz. container sour cream

Add dry cake mix to a large bowl. Cut in butter with 2 knives or a
pastry cutter until crumbly. Mix in coconut. Pat mixture lightly into
a greased 13"x9" baking pan, building up the sides a little. Bake at
350 degrees for 10 minutes; remove from oven. Arrange apples over
warm crust. Mix sugar and cinnamon in a cup; sprinkle over apples. In
a small bowl, whisk together egg and sour cream; drizzle over apples.
Topping will not completely cover apples. Bake at 350 degrees for
25 minutes, or until edges are lightly golden. Do not overbake. Serve
warm or cold. Makes 12 servings.

If it's been too long since you've visited with good friends,
why not host a casual holiday get-together? Potlucks are
so easy to plan...everyone brings along their favorite dish
to share. It's all about food, fun and fellowship!

Granny Shirey's Fresh Apple Cake

Susan Butterworth
Harper, TX

For as long as I can remember, my mom made this special cake at Christmas from a recipe passed down from her own mother, our Granny Shirey. Our family doesn't care much for fruitcake, so Mom made this cake for us. It's really good with a cup of coffee after all the hustle & bustle of Christmas Eve, after all are gone to bed, and before the celebrations begin.

2 c. sugar
3/4 c. oil
2 eggs, well beaten
2 T. vanilla extract
juice of 1 lemon
1 t. salt

3 c. all-purpose flour
1-1/4 t. baking soda
3 c. Granny Smith apples,
   peeled, cored and chopped
1-1/2 c. chopped walnuts
   or pecans

In a large bowl, combine sugar, oil, eggs, vanilla, lemon juice and salt. Beat well and set aside. In a separate bowl, blend flour and baking soda; add to sugar mixture and stir well. Fold in apples and nuts. Pour batter into a greased and floured tube pan. Bake at 325 degrees for 1-1/2 hours. Makes 12 servings.

Turn a Bundt® cake into a holiday wreath. Drizzle with frosting, then sprinkle chopped green and red candied cherries over the top. Twist a long strip of red fruit leather into a jaunty bow to complete the wreath.

Sweets
OF THE SEASON

Cranberry Nut Bread

Liz Blackstone
Racine, WI

My Aunt Joan gave me this quick bread recipe. It's equally good at breakfast or alongside a roast turkey.

2 c. all-purpose flour
1 c. sugar
1-1/2 t. baking powder
1/2 t. baking soda
1 t. salt
2 T. shortening

1 egg, beaten
1 T. orange zest
3/4 c. orange juice
1-1/2 c. fresh or frozen
    cranberries, coarsely chopped
1/2 c. chopped walnuts

In a large bowl, mix together flour, sugar, baking powder, baking soda and salt. Add shortening, egg, orange zest and juice; mix until well blended. Fold in cranberries and nuts. Spread batter evenly in a greased 9"x5" loaf pan. Bake at 350 degrees for 55 minutes, or until a toothpick tests clean. Cool in pan on a wire rack for 15 minutes. Remove from pan; cool. Wrap in aluminum foil or plastic wrap; store overnight before slicing. Makes one loaf.

Grandpa Weber's Banana Bread

Kris Kellis
Salisbury, NC

Whenever Grandpa came for dinner, he brought a loaf of this wonderful banana bread tucked under his arm.

1/3 c. shortening
3/4 c. brown sugar, packed
2 eggs, beaten
1 c. ripe bananas, mashed
1-1/2 c. all-purpose flour

1 t. baking soda
1 t. salt
1/2 c. milk
Optional: 1/2 c. chopped walnuts

In a large bowl, beat shortening and brown sugar thoroughly. Add eggs and bananas; beat until light. In a separate bowl, sift together flour, baking soda and salt. Add flour mixture and milk alternately to shortening mixture; beat after each addition until smooth. Fold in nuts, if using. Pour batter into a greased 9"x5" loaf pan. Bake at 350 degrees for one hour and 5 minutes, or until a toothpick tests done. Turn out of pan; cool on a wire rack. Wrap in aluminum foil or plastic wrap; store overnight before slicing. Makes one loaf.

Red Velvet Cake Trifle

Colleen Ramsey
Meredosia, IL

My husband's favorite cake is red velvet. So for his birthday, I came up with this delicious recipe, and he loved it. Perfect for Christmas parties too...it makes enough for a crowd!

16-1/2 oz. pkg. red velvet
   cake mix
1 t. vanilla extract
2-1/2 c. milk
3-1/2 oz. pkg. instant
   cheesecake pudding mix

3-1/2 oz. pkg. instant white
   chocolate pudding mix
8-oz. container frozen whipped
   topping, thawed
Optional: 4 strawberries, hulled
   and thinly sliced

Prepare and bake cake mix according to package directions, adding vanilla to batter. Cool completely in pan on a wire rack. Cut cake into one-inch cubes; set aside. In a large bowl, combine milk and both pudding mixes. Beat with an electric mixer on low speed for 2 minutes, or until thickened. Let stand for 2 minutes, or until soft set. Fold in whipped topping. To assemble, place 1/2 of cake cubes in a clear glass trifle bowl; spread 1/2 of pudding over top. Repeat layering. Garnish with strawberries, if desired. Cover and chill until serving time. Serves 16.

Old-fashioned favorites like a vintage sled or pair of ice skates by the front door are a sweet welcome for friends. Tie on evergreen boughs, pine cones & red berry sprigs for cheery color.

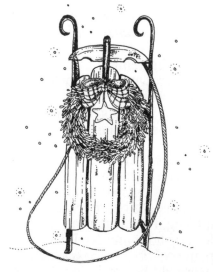

Sweets
OF THE SEASON

Peanut Butter Brownie Trifle
Lynnette Jones
East Flat Rock, NC

*This really feeds a lot of folks! It's a good dessert
to make if you are having company.*

18-oz. pkg. brownie mix
3 c. milk
5.1-oz. pkg. instant vanilla
    pudding mix
2 t. vanilla extract

1/2 c. creamy peanut butter
2 c. frozen whipped topping,
    thawed
1-1/2 12-oz. pkgs. mini peanut
    butter cups

Prepare and bake brownies according to package directions. Cool
completely in pan on a wire rack. Cut brownies into one-inch cubes;
set aside. Combine milk and pudding mix in a large bowl. Beat with an
electric mixer on medium speed for 2 minutes. Cover and refrigerate for
10 to 15 minutes. Fold vanilla, peanut butter and 1-1/2 cups whipped
topping into pudding; set aside. Cut peanut butter cups into 4 pieces
each. In a large clear glass trifle bowl, layer 1/3 each of brownie cubes
and pudding; add 1/4 of peanut butter cups. Repeat layering twice.
Spread with remaining topping; garnish with remaining peanut butter
cups. Cover and chill until serving time. Serves 12 to 14.

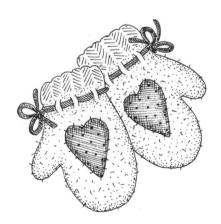

Pack a small plastic bag full of treats and pop it inside
a mitten for a sweet holiday gift. Shop after the season
to find mittens on sale for next year!

Mocha Snowball Cookies

Jean DePerna
Fairport, NY

I always make these cookies at Christmas to take to work. The one year I decided to change things up and make something different... well, let's say my co-workers were not happy. I had to make some and bring them in after our party!

1 c. butter, softened
1/2 c. sugar
2 t. vanilla extract
1-3/4 c. all-purpose flour
1/4 c. baking cocoa

2 t. instant coffee granules
1/2 t. salt
2 c. walnuts or almonds, finely
   chopped
Garnish: powdered sugar

In a large bowl, blend together butter, sugar and vanilla until smooth. Stir in flour, cocoa, coffee and salt until well mixed; fold in nuts. Wrap dough in plastic wrap and refrigerate for at least one hour. Roll dough into walnut-size balls. Arrange on lightly greased or parchment paper-lined baking sheets, 2 inches apart. Bake at 325 degrees for 15 minutes, or until tops of cookies are firm to the touch. Cool for 15 minutes; roll in powdered sugar to coat. Makes 3 dozen.

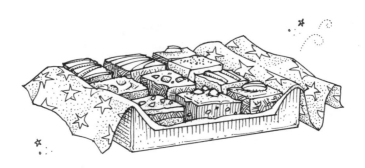

It's the season for sharing! Set aside a few cookies from each batch you bake. In no time at all, you can make up a platter of assorted cookies to drop off at a neighborhood firehouse, family shelter or retirement home.

Sweets
OF THE SEASON

Holiday Nutmeg Cookies

Mary Kay Hahn
Willoughby, OH

These have been a favorite family cookie for years.
They are easy to make and share for a cookie exchange.

2 T. red or green colored sugar
3/4 t. nutmeg, divided
1-1/2 c. all-purpose flour
3/4 c. sugar
1 t. cream of tartar

1/2 t. baking soda
1/8 t. salt
1/2 c. butter, softened
1 egg, beaten
1 t. vanilla extract

Combine colored sugar and 1/4 teaspoon nutmeg in a small bowl; set aside. In a separate large bowl, combine flour, sugar, cream of tartar, baking soda, salt and remaining nutmeg; stir together. Add butter, egg and vanilla. Beat with an electric mixer on low speed until well mixed. Form dough into one-inch balls; roll in sugar-nutmeg mixture. Place on ungreased baking sheets, 2 inches apart. Bake at 400 degrees for 10 to 12 minutes, until firm. Cool on wire racks. Makes about 3 dozen.

Treats a busy mom would love anytime! Spoon scoops of cookie dough onto baking sheets and freeze. After the dough is frozen, toss it into a plastic zipping bag labeled with the cookie name and baking instructions.

Sunshine Pineapple Cookies

Judy Henfey
Cibolo, TX

This recipe came from a cookbook my second-grade class made for our mothers at Christmas in 1973. The print is fading, but not the memories of our favorite teacher, Miss Wolfgang. I had forgotten about this little cookbook until I opened an old box that was in storage. My late mom had kept it for me after all these years!

1 c. butter
1-1/2 c. sugar
1 egg, beaten
8-1/2 oz. can crushed pineapple,
   drained

1/2 c. chopped pecans
3-1/2 c. all-purpose flour
1 t. baking soda
1/2 t. salt
1/4 t. nutmeg

In a large bowl, beat butter, sugar and egg with an electric mixer on medium speed until very light. Beat in pineapple and pecans on low speed; set aside. In a separate bowl, sift together flour, baking soda, salt and nutmeg. Beat flour mixture into butter mixture. Drop batter by heaping tablespoons onto lightly greased baking sheets, 2-1/2 inches apart. Bake at 375 degrees for 10 to 15 minutes, until golden. Remove to a wire rack; cool. Makes 3 dozen.

A one-gallon glass apothecary jar makes a great cookie jar. Personalize it by using a glass paint pen to add a personal message and hearts or swirls, just for fun.

Sweets
OF THE SEASON

Old-Fashioned Mincemeat Bars

Shirley Howie
Foxboro, MA

This is a very old recipe that has been handed down in my mother's family for at least three generations. It brings back wonderful memories of our family holidays spent together, as we always made these for Thanksgiving and Christmas.

2 c. old-fashioned oats,
    uncooked
1-1/2 c. all-purpose flour
3/4 c. sugar

1/3 c. molasses
1/2 t. salt
3/4 c. butter
27-oz. jar mincemeat

Combine oats, flour, sugar, molasses and salt in a large bowl. Using 2 knives or a pastry blender, cut in butter until mixture resembles coarse crumbs. Press half of oat mixture into a greased 9"x9" baking pan. Spoon mincemeat over top; crumble remaining oat mixture evenly over mincemeat. Bake at 350 degrees for 25 minutes, or until lightly golden. Cool completely in pan on a wire rack; cut into bars. Makes 16 bars.

Quick Fruitcake

Julie Ann Perkins
Anderson, IN

This easy recipe will give you extra time to spend wrapping gifts or simply relaxing by a warm fire. Also makes great gifts for neighbors...make ahead so they can enjoy on Christmas Day.

1-1/2 lbs. mixed candied fruit
3-1/2 oz. can flaked coconut
1 lb. pecan halves or pieces

14-oz. can sweetened condensed
    milk

Combine all ingredients in a large bowl; mix well. Spread into a greased 9"x5" loaf pan. Bake at 250 degrees for 2 hours. Cool; turn out of pan. Cut into slices; cut slices in half, if desired. Makes one to 2 dozen servings.

Grandma Taylor's Cranberry Cookies

Sara Hope
Tillamook, OR

My grandmother shared a raisin cookie recipe with me 20 years ago that had come from her own great-grandma. I changed the raisins to cranberries...they've been a family favorite ever since.

1 c. butter, softened
1 c. brown sugar, packed
1 c. sugar
2 eggs, beaten
3-1/2 c. all-purpose flour
1 t. baking powder

2 t. baking soda
1 c. sweetened dried cranberries
1 c. chopped pecans or walnuts
1-1/2 c. old-fashioned oats, uncooked

In a large bowl, blend together butter, sugars and eggs. Add flour, baking powder and baking soda; mix well. Fold in remaining ingredients. Scoop dough by rounded tablespoons onto non-stick or parchment paper-lined baking sheets. Bake at 350 degrees for 9 to 12 minutes, until golden. Makes 2 dozen.

To keep a potted Christmas poinsettia fresh, place it in a sunny spot, away from cold drafts. Water whenever the soil on top feels dry...it'll continue to bloom for weeks.

Amaretto Biscotti Cookies

Judy Borecky
Escondido, CA

These cookies are perfect for dunking. I love the taste of amaretto, so I came up with this original recipe to share with my family, especially during the holidays. They're perfect for gift giving...and you will never have to buy biscotti cookies again...enjoy!

1 c. butter, softened
2 c. sugar
1/2 c. brown sugar, packed
1/4 c. amaretto liqueur
2 eggs, beaten
3-1/2 c. all-purpose flour

1 t. baking soda
1 t. salt
6-oz. pkg. semi-sweet chocolate chips
1 c. sweetened flaked coconut

In a large bowl, beat butter and sugars until light in color. Add amaretto and eggs; beat until blended and set aside. In a small bowl, whisk together flour, baking soda and salt. Add flour mixture to butter mixture; blend well. Fold in chocolate chips and coconut. With a small ice cream scoop, add dough to ungreased baking sheets, about 2 tablespoons per cookie. Bake at 350 degrees for about 12 minutes, until lightly golden. Cool cookies on baking sheets for 5 minutes; remove to wire racks. Makes 4 to 5 dozen.

At dessert time, set out whipped cream and shakers of cinnamon and cocoa for coffee drinkers. Tea drinkers will love a basket of special teas with honey and lemon slices.

Crantastic Holiday Fudge

Jennifer Day
Cresson, TX

This is the perfect fudge for little ones to help make...it's so easy and fun! When it's done, that first bite is sure to brighten your day.

12-oz. pkg. semi-sweet
   chocolate chips
1 c. milk chocolate chips
14-oz. can sweetened
   condensed milk

1 t. vanilla extract
1 c. sweetened dried
   cranberries
1-1/2 c. mini marshmallows

Line an 8"x8" baking pan with aluminum foil, extending foil over the edges; set aside. Combine all chocolate chips in a large microwave-safe bowl. Microwave for 1-1/2 minutes on 50% power; stir. If needed, microwave for 15 seconds at a time on 50% power, just until chips are melted when stirred. Stir in remaining ingredients. Immediately spread into prepared pan. Refrigerate for 2 hours. Use aluminum foil to lift out of pan; cut into small squares. Makes 4 to 5 dozen.

Fudgy Buttons

Crystal Branstrom
Russell, PA

I've been making this recipe for years. My children enjoyed these little morsels when they were small, and now my granddaughter Cricket loves them too. Better make a double batch!

2 T. butter, melted
1-1/2 t. baking cocoa
1/2 c. powdered sugar

1/2 t. milk
2 T. creamy peanut butter

In a large bowl, combine butter and cocoa; stir in powdered sugar. Add milk; stir until smooth. Add peanut butter; mix well. Roll into small balls; place on wax paper. Flatten tops with your thumb or a fork. Let stand until set. Makes 15 small candies.

Strawberries & Cream Fudge

Beverly Mahorney
Cynthiana, KY

One of my most treasured memories is of making Christmas candy with my mother. We would set aside a day to make batch after batch of beautiful confections. This recipe is my take on marshmallow creme fudge, using mini marshmallows instead.

3/4 c. butter
3 c. sugar
2/3 c. evaporated milk
12-oz. pkg. white
    chocolate chips

1-1/2 c. mini marshmallows
1 T. strawberry extract
12 to 15 drops red food
    coloring

Line a 13"x9" baking pan with aluminum foil, allowing extra for handles. Spray with non-stick vegetable spray; set aside. In a heavy saucepan, combine butter, sugar and evaporated milk. Bring to a boil over medium heat, stirring constantly. Boil for 5 minutes; remove from heat. Add chocolate chips and marshmallows; stir until melted. Remove one cup of fudge to a bowl; set aside. Add extract and food coloring to remaining fudge in saucepan; mix well and spread into prepared pan. Dollop reserved white fudge on top; swirl with a knife to marble. Let stand until firm. Lift out fudge by the aluminum foil handles onto a cutting board; cut into squares. Makes about 3 pounds.

Fudge keeps well and makes a wonderful gift! Since it isn't prone to crumbling, it's a perfect choice for mailing to loved ones in faraway places. Wrap tightly in plastic wrap before boxing it up.

Index

Index

Index

Find Gooseberry Patch
wherever you are!

www.gooseberrypatch.com

Call us toll-free at 1·800·854·6673

handknit mittens　strings of popcorn

homemade candy

sugar cookies

holly & mistletoe

letters to Santa

paper snowflakes　curling ribbons

U.S. to Metric Recipe Equivalents

Volume Measurements

1/4 teaspoon	1 mL
1/2 teaspoon	2 mL
1 teaspoon	5 mL
1 tablespoon = 3 teaspoons	15 mL
2 tablespoons = 1 fluid ounce	30 mL
1/4 cup	60 mL
1/3 cup	75 mL
1/2 cup = 4 fluid ounces	125 mL
1 cup = 8 fluid ounces	250 mL
2 cups = 1 pint =16 fluid ounces	500 mL
4 cups = 1 quart	1 L

Weights

1 ounce	30 g
4 ounces	120 g
8 ounces	225 g
16 ounces = 1 pound	450 g

Oven Temperatures

300° F	150° C
325° F	160° C
350° F	180° C
375° F	190° C
400° F	200° C
450° F	230° C

Baking Pan Sizes

Square		
8x8x2 inches	2 L = 20x20x5 cm	
9x9x2 inches	2.5 L = 23x23x5 cm	
Rectangular		
13x9x2 inches	3.5 L = 33x23x5 cm	

Loaf		
9x5x3 inches	2 L = 23x13x7 cm	
Round		
8x1-1/2 inches	1.2 L = 20x4 cm	
9x1-1/2 inches	1.5 L = 23x4 cm	